You Are the
CAKE

Discover your essence, and Revel in the Sweetness!

GEETANJALI ARUNKUMAR

ISBN: 9781092980890

I dedicate this book to my children, Amit and Priyanka, whose love shines bright, and to my darling mother, Jamuna, for her unconditional love and guidance.

CONTENTS

"Cake is happiness! If you know the way of the cake, you know the way of happiness! If you have a cake in front of you, you should not look any further for joy!"

— C. JoyBell C.

Chapter 1

Know You Are the Cake

I followed the wafting aroma and opened the door to the bakery where varieties of cakes caught my eye, displayed in the glass showcase. I looked with delight, feeling my nose twitch and my mouth water. From the pink swirl of the raspberry cheesecake; to the bundt cake that looked like a beautiful, big donut; to the chocolate-and-white yule log with a checkerboard pattern, my senses felt stunned. Then there was the brandied fruit cake and the flourless round lemon cake. Each of these cakes stood tall in its own gorgeous uniqueness, distinct and individual.

Look at all of us. Aren't we like these fantastic cakes, given a chance to be unique and distinct, each filled with layers of our personality? We are a blend of mind, body, subconscious, conscious, spirit, soul, and energy. We sift and blend the ingredients to make beautiful ribbons of "batter," fluffy and light. We bake the batter into any shape or form we choose it to be, albeit with imperfections, just as we would prepare a moist, luscious cake. We blend together an individualized self. We are every bit as extraordinary as those fantastic cakes inside the showcase. Realizing that, and accepting ourselves, is crucial to personal happiness. And hence derives my title for this book: *You Are the Cake*!

Yes, you are the stable and steady substance like the cake, standing tall in the light of happiness, gratitude, joy, and love. When we blend the ingredients, they are integrated into a whole, as one. We all face fears, doubt, and despair and tend to express our negative feelings from time to time. Life cannot always be about sweetness, but we learn to accept, be aware of, and observe the negative feelings. We learn to be cognizant of our feelings and thoughts. We go through the twists and turns presented to us, make changes, and train our brains to hold onto more positive thoughts. We learn to be aware of all the ingredients of our body and mind and bring them in harmony to live a life of ease, peace, and love.

You may say "I am the cake" and still mistakenly believe that the icing, sprinkles, decorations, or glaze are terribly important, but they are not the essence of the cake. They are not *you*. You are the cake itself—the essence, the substance—whether that is airy, dense, moist, creamy, zesty or zingy. When you are filled with love and have blended the ingredients well, then you are the true essence, and the externals that surround you—icing, sprinkles, candles—merely enhance the inner beauty of you.

2

All of us, as young children knew we were "the cake." We were curious, spontaneous, adventurous, carefree, fearless, and unconditionally loved. If we fell, we got up, dusted ourselves off, and continued forward with ebullient enthusiasm. We were free of stress or worries, but then we grew up and found ourselves faced with responsibilities, realities, and goals. If you once knew that you are the cake, then surely you can learn to reawaken the inner child in you and live your life as that carefree youngster. How to do that is the topic of this book.

Life is a journey of happiness and struggles for each one of us. For some, it is the trivial things that seem overwhelming. For others, life brings on a hurricane of difficult times. Eventually we realize that we need to take charge of ourselves and find a solution to live a happier and more peaceful life, a life where we are authentically true to ourselves.

MY STORY

The ideas and suggestions I share in this book are based on my own experience, so let me start by telling you what happened in my life that drew me back to finally remembering that I am the cake. I was happy as a child and until my mid-twenties. I enjoyed my career and kept fit by playing tennis. Then I moved to another country, had problems with my visa status, and was denied the opportunity to work. The lack of financial resources, living in a high-crime area, and loneliness, threw me off-balance. I was stuck at home for over two years wondering why I was in this state. My mind chatter and negative self-talk brought on more worked-up feelings. The authentic, true me began to fade.

Fearful of what others would say or think, I did not confide in anyone about my feelings. I was diagnosed with a medical issue. Even though we moved as a married couple to a sunnier state, my visa status still did not allow me to venture into the workforce. I was unable to meet my parents for three years, my husband worked long hours, and I was unhappy and alone. This is not what I had pictured my life was going to be. Inside, I was frustrated and angry. Everything looked so gloomy and bleak.

I was being sucked into a deep abyss of pain, insomnia, migraines, digestive issues, and fatigue. The ache of not knowing what was happening to me and why, brought me deeper into a pit of anguish and bitterness. Most of the time I felt sick. My life, which I had cherished in my youth, brimming with potential happiness, seemed to have gone up in flames. How would I be able to bring up my two beautiful toddlers in my mental and physical state?

I went in search of a doctor to help me. After four years with no answers, one doctor told me I had a chronic, invisible, lifelong illness. One where not much research was being carried out and one that the medical community believed was "psychological." I sat in the doctor's office in shock and disbelief. What little was left of my aspirations and dreams was swept away by this news in a tidal wave of grief.

But I had a family to care for. There was no time to dwell on my sadness. I continued being the best mother I could be, gathered up my courage and my love for the young ones, and pulled myself together to give them the happiness they so deserved. But didn't I deserve happiness, too? My culture had taught me that I should give to my family and others, but I never learned that I had to give to myself. I didn't understand that if I took care of myself, and became kind to myself, I could radiate more love and happiness to others. We are taught these limited beliefs which become the framework of who we are. We need to be ourselves and break these embedded patterns and move to a better place in our lives. We must let go of the past and live in the present moment.

I read more about my mysterious, debilitating, chronic illness. With more certainty than ever, I knew I had to make a life for our family and not be hindered by upheavals or adversities. Over the years I have been bedridden, housebound for months, confined to a wheelchair, and unable to carry out the most basic personal functions (such as showering). But with the deep knowing that I could do it, I carried on. I knew that my optimistic vision, courage, resilience, and belief in myself would get me through the difficult times. I stood tall, ready to face anything dealt to me. The will to live and the commitment I had for my loved ones, led me through the arduous times to reach this point where I am now at peace and filled with love. It has taken me this life journey to understand that we are not what others see us as, but how we look at and care for ourselves.

The secrets of life unfolded in front of my eyes like a cocoon metamorphosing into a beautiful butterfly. With the air beneath my wings, I was released and lifted into an extraordinary journey of self-knowledge, love, and becoming the creator of my own life. Most of all I learned to be in the finite moment, integrating the lessons from both my adverse and happy experiences. I am here to rejoice with every breath as I marvel at the precious gift of life.

I am fortunate that twenty years later, there is finally some validation for this chronic illness, with research and more funding. Could I wait twenty years to get better and happier, or would I take my destiny into my own hands? I made my choice. How about you? Will you decide to make your life, to reach your full potential, to live with more peace and harmony? To be who you were meant to be?

Life to me has been like a gushing river with some overflows on the muddy banks. It sometimes glistens and shines and other times rages with no control. All of us go through the ups and downs. Master Sheng-Yen Lu, the wise Buddhist monk, says it beautifully: "Be soft in your practice. Think of the method (life) as a fine silvery stream, not a raging waterfall. Follow the stream. Have faith in its course. It will go on its way, meandering here, trickling there. It will find the grooves, the cracks, the crevices. Just follow it. Never let it out of your sight. It will take you there."

We all will go through rigor and challenges, and in this book you will learn techniques and simple strategies to help you deal with them with ease and confidence. You will come to realize that you are the creator of your life and that you can attract an abundance of love, wealth, health, and anything you desire.

Let's take the first step in becoming aware that we have embedded patterns or specific conditioning which we need to disarm. Human nature is such that we blame ourselves and turn to self-criticism, analyzing and ruminating in our negative thoughts. Caring for and accepting ourselves is critical to our mental, physical, and spiritual health. Be aware, observe, and know with certainty that you are "the cake"—marvelous, unique, and gifted.

If you are reading this book, you have taken a most essential step in deciding you want to make a change. You are acknowledging that you are *worthy* of the difference. We all search for happiness and peace. That search is ingrained in us. We can learn to be grateful and live as the highest version of ourselves. How do we change the hardships into loving, joyful moments? How do we create love to overcome the troubled times and to make impossibilities into possibilities?

I encourage you to read on and learn the simple ways that you can genuinely realize, reawaken, and be who you truly were meant to be. Let's integrate and blend the ingredients to make it happen ... to be that distinctive cake that is you.

MIND PATTERNS

Bruce Lee Tao of Jeet Kune Do has observed how our thought patterns and life patterns can function like a cage: "Set patterns, incapable of adaptability, of pliability, only offer a better cage. Truth is outside of all patterns."

How many of us are aware of our thought patterns? Are you conscious of the inner critic in you, the negative self- talk you sometimes fixate your thoughts on? Do you feel that this mind chatter constantly repeats, keeping you stuck in a past way of thinking or worn-out belief?

We all have thoughts floating in and out of our minds, and these create positive or negative neural pathways. They form into our habits, patterns, and beliefs. Wouldn't we all like to disarm the disempowering thoughts and replace them with positive ones? We deserve to let the volume of the mean voice in our heads be turned down, and to increase the intensity of our empowering thoughts.

Maya is listening to John. It goes like this, "Every time I go to work, I get the flu, and I get so angry at these people who walk around passing on their bugs to me. It's so hard to pay the rent, and why don't they pay me more for all I do?" Gasping with emotion, he continues, "Did you hear that the house next door was robbed, and the man had a heart attack when the thieves tied him up?" Maya looks on and wants to escape from all this negativity but continues listening, knowing that John has what she calls "drama patterns." She stands politely listening but not absorbing or taking in his negativity. John is the kind of person who, when things are calm, always feels an inner urge telling him calm is not the norm and that he needs to create some drama to feel good within.

There are those who have a pattern of always complaining that they do not have the finances to go out to eat, travel, or enjoy themselves once in a while. Why is this? Their pattern of mind chatter tells them that having money is not right. It doesn't feel comfortable, to them, to be abundant. Unaware of their internal mind pattern that whispers, "I don't have money and will never have it," they go through life believing they are not worth having money and financial freedom.

Other people have a fear that things will always go wrong regardless of what they try. They feel nothing ever turns out right. They don't feel important and despise everyone, and no one seems to value them.

All these attitudes are examples of different negative mind patterns. What mind patterns do you have that you would like to change?

Get yourself a blank notebook, and let it be your journal as you work your way through this book. Think about the question you just read, and contemplate it quietly. Then write your answer in the journal. For your convenience you can download and print out the journaling questions in a worksheet format. Please refer to the Recommended Resources section at the end of the book to access it.

Contemplating and journaling as you go through these chapters will tap the wisdom and knowingness that lies within you at your deepest, intuitive level. The answers for your life are not mine to give. I only can share my experiences and point you in the right direction. You need to look inside yourself for the truth that will set you free. And that requires work and contemplation—and journaling! Writing down your thoughts is much more powerful than simply sitting and thinking. That's because writing focuses the mind. It forces vague thoughts to become specific. So before you read any further, if you haven't already done so, get your hands on the notebook that is going to be your journal!

Now let us return to the topic of mind patterns. Some of us have happy mind patterns that lead us to be aware of the miracles and the goodness in our lives, receiving them with gratitude. Such people also go through difficult times but live in the moment and are able to acknowledge the beauty within and around them. As Rudyard Kipling challenged in a famous poem: "If you can meet with triumph and disaster and treat those two impostors just the same ..."

There have to be adverse times for us to appreciate the good times. We have to understand both the positive and negative to come out shining brighter and happier. Many of us have happy patterns, and here is a scenario that you may relate to:

Tom came home to his wife, Maria, and gave her a small bouquet of flowers. She gave him a big hug, thanking him with her words and a smile. Maria had also returned from work and had cooked a hot meal for Tom and the kids. As they sat around the dining table, the oldest child was delighted to get his favorite dish of chicken. He thanked his mom by smiling and appreciating the scrumptious meal. Maria was recognized for her efforts and felt contented. At the end of the dinner, Tom loaded up the dishwasher for his wife, as the kids had to get back to their homework.

This shows a pattern of love, depicted in different ways, such as Tom's surprise gift or his act of service in cleaning up the dishes. Maria had made a hot meal for the family—also an act of service showing love—and it was nice to hear the child expressing appreciation. When children are aware of love and approval from their parents, they respond positively.

Some people have positive mind patterns about money and success. They tell themselves that they are successful and always do well in their business or career. They seem to be predetermined to do well financially, because the internal programming is positive. Some people have positive mind patterns about health. They tell themselves and believe that they have radiant health and feel good about themselves. They have wired themselves to stay well.

Your subconscious mind—that inner, intuitive part of the mind ... the deeper layer, which handles your actions and feelings—is like a computer. It receives messages from the conscious mind and retrieves and stores extensive data. Your subconscious mind takes all the data and puts it into patterns which help form your self-image, whether it be positive or negative.

Psychological research shows us ways of creating a positive mindset. Since childhood, our mental and behavioral patterns started to get formed, influencing everything from the way we react to stressful situations to the way we walk and the way we brush our hair. We form steadfast patterns at different stages of our life. These may be stimulated by the environment, parents, peers, or the media.

Sue, a young teen, was confrontational with friends and spoke poorly of them behind their backs. Social situations that caused conflict could have been harmonized with an open and positive attitude. But Sue was used to hearing her parents talk about their colleagues, friends, and neighbors in a harsh and judgmental way. This habit brushed off on Sue, who grew up displaying the same behavior pattern.

Many of us recognize our negative habits and mind patterns and genuinely dislike them, but feel we have to go along with them. We tend to follow societal rules and norms, sometimes moving with the wrong circle of friends, reading upsetting gossip in the tabloids, being swayed by parents' expectations, or responding to programming by an agenda-driven media. We may start to hate ourselves. We feel trapped in the chains of the patterns we are in, and are keen to break free and be ourselves without upsetting the delicate balance of emotion that we are used to.

If we become aware that we need to make a change and *shift* to more encouraging thoughts, then we are on track to accepting ourselves for who we are. So how do we interrupt habitual negative patterns of thought and replace them with positive ones? We integrate the good and the bad by changing the imperfection, reprogramming the subconscious mind to learn a new pattern or habit in its place. For example, when I am home and get tempted by the cookies, I move toward them, but next to them I have healthier walnuts available as an alternative. My conscious mind directs me to the cookies which always give me a sugar high (my old habit or pattern), but I trained my conscious mind in a short length of time to go for the healthier choice. I became aware of the pattern I didn't want and learned to replace it with something that enabled me to feel better and care for myself.

Leo was a chain smoker who started the smoking habit not meaning to harm himself. Over time he came to see that the habit was destructive. His friends told him to "just quit cold turkey," but his neurotransmitters fired to tell him that was not possible. His brain was wired to have a cigarette in times of stress to feel calm. His emotional side liked the feeling of smoking and feeling less worked up. But the unrest of shame told him that he had to break this bad habit which had a hold on him. It affected his physical health and emotions and gave him a feeling of powerlessness. What should he do?

Could he slowly reduce the number of cigarettes he smoked and, in their place, eat a few carrot sticks? Leo could carry these with him, but having carrot sticks with him at all times could become another habit. Leo joined a support group, where he learned that picturing himself as a nonsmoker would help him to become one. He began to picture himself as a person with clothes that did not smell of smoke. He imagined his car and house feeling cleaner, and the air more comfortable to breathe.

Leo was told that it's very hard to just break a bad habit, and that the way to change the pattern is to establish a new good habit in the bad habit's place. So Leo decided to replace his habit of smoking twenty cigarettes a day with the habit

11

of smoking fifteen a day, and as time went by, he reduced the number still further. Slowly he found himself smoking less.

With the help of his support group, Leo learned that it's okay to be upset and feel compassion for himself for the uncomfortable process he was going through. Leo's subconscious was ingrained in the pattern of smoking to release his anxiety. The new habit of smoking less was making his life better by substituting a new practice for an old one. He took incremental steps, confronting the habit, bringing awareness to the situation, having loving kindness for himself, pausing and letting out his frustrations when things were not moving in the desired direction, and picturing himself how he would be without smoking. Most of all, he chose to replace the old habit which had become dysfunctional with a new pattern which made him live a healthier and better quality of life and so empowered him. In time he reduced his intake to one cigarette a day, and then none a day. Leo today is more robust, happier, and in step with his choices. He lives a more enhanced and meaningful life.

The bad habits that don't serve us anymore are replaced by more desired ones. Like the river that once was polluted with toxins, where plants and fish were dying but where now the water has cleared and life is thriving again, we also can clear the pollutants from our thoughts and begin to act in ways that support our happiness.

Life changes when we make the change. Think positively about yourself and your circumstances. Replace the bad with the good. Find good in the smallest of things, and realize with gratitude what you have, and who you are.

It is with such vulnerability that I write to you. As a homemaker in our society, I did not feel worthy and felt sensitive when people ignored me at social events. I assumed they thought I was uninteresting or not intelligent enough to take part in conversations. I volunteered in my children's school, read newspapers, and could speak on many subjects but could not go out and work. I developed a pattern of not liking myself, and every time a small incident occurred where I felt unrecognized, I heard my inner voice say that I had been insulted. This limiting belief about myself was sabotaging the way I lived. I could feel the pain and anguish, but I carried on, knowing that this unworthy feeling needed to be changed. I found a way to let go of what other people thought and learned to appreciate and love myself.

Do you feel at times that you have little value? I had admitted this feeling to myself, but the voice within me kept saying that it was not true. I was scared and wanted to change the bad feeling. Every time there was a sensitive situation, I decided to let it go and not analyze it further. I repeated to myself that I was worthy. Now that I love myself, and have a greater understanding of me, I am more confident and send out the vibrations of happiness and self-esteem to others around me.

I let go of the hurt of the past about my relationships, love, wealth, and self-esteem. I started with a clean slate, and I do not hold a grudge or hurt anyone or anything. I have reduced my expectations and judgments of myself and others. I send love to all and receive it back tenfold. Letting go of your limiting beliefs and embedded patterns leads to more happiness. Have faith in the love you have for yourself, and do not stand in the way of others succeeding, too. Let go of the envy and other negative emotions.

Try to be aware of the negative pattern or the repetitive habit when it is playing out, and you will realize that you do not need it anymore. Stop the pattern, and in its place, rewrite a new one that is beneficial to you. You will experience what it is to be free from the habits that hold you down. Choose a natural state of joy and well-being.

Society teaches us that we should not love ourselves. Loving oneself is seen as egotistical, narcissistic, and selfish. But what happens when you love someone? You care, you are kind, and you do anything and everything so that they are happy. Now consider yourself: would it be wrong to do the same for you? Is it wrong to show yourself some kindness?

Loving yourself doesn't mean taking selfies or posting your status on social media. It's the way we treat ourselves. You should treat yourself the same kind way that you treat someone you love. Treat yourself with the same compassion until your cup runneth over. That way there is enough love to radiate out to others.

How can we give ourselves love if we are held back by the embedded patterns and ingrained habits which tell us we are being selfish to love ourselves? Go on, thrive, and find your inner gift and potential. Live with faith, in loving kindness for yourself. You are worth it and richly deserve to be loved. Break the pattern of fear of loving yourself. Don't give a second thought to what people may think of you. You are not conceited, vain, or arrogant because you treat yourself well. It is time to live your life!

Questions for Your Journal

1. *What negative mind patterns (negative mind chatter, negative attitude, or self-talk) do you notice repeating within you? Examine your attitudes in terms of the various life areas: health, wealth, occupation, relationships, and spirituality. After identifying a negative attitude, write it down in the form of a sentence.*

2. *What negative feelings arise within you when you think that negative thought? Write down an answer for each of the attitudes you identified in question #1.*

3. *For each of the attitudes you have identified, rewrite the sentence in terms of the mind pattern you would like to have in its place.*

4. *Next to each positive mind pattern you have written, write the positive feeling you expect to feel when you replace the negative pattern with the positive one.*

5. *How committed are you to turning your negative mind patterns into positive ones? Grade your commitment on a scale of one to ten, with ten representing a very strong commitment. In the chapters that follow you will learn how to rewire your brain, removing destructive attitudes and replacing them with life-supporting ones!*

Chapter 2

Luscious Cake Layers

Do you let your peers, family, media, or society make you feel that you should not accept who you are, that you are not okay the way you are? Can you imagine feeling like a child again, free of the mind patterns that tell you not to love yourself? Are you willing to give yourself a chance to realize that you are good? Are you willing to do the work it takes to change the mind patterns that cause you to hate, criticize, judge, and push yourself to the point of perfectionism?

If your answer to the above questions is yes, it is right that you are here, reading this book. So, let us talk more about this love of self and why it is so important. How does it come about? How can you learn to be your own best friend?

Though society may regard loving oneself as egotistical, narcissistic, or selfish, it is the secret ingredient of happiness and living a purposeful life. Loving ourselves is an absolute necessity. We need to learn who we are, both internally and externally, and to be in love with that. If only we were taught this at a young age! Instead, in our consumerist and unyielding, fast-paced society, we are conditioned to believe that we are not good enough.

We are taught that it is conceited and self-absorbed to rightly voice that we love ourselves. Society approves a mother or father loving their child, children loving their parents, and siblings loving each other and their extended families. We are applauded for making such efforts of love, and that is as it should be. But is it enough? Can we honestly give genuine love to anyone else if we don't have love for ourselves first?

Society also teaches us that we need someone else to complete us. Aren't we enough by ourselves? Magazines, TV, and movies all convey the message that we need something or someone outside of ourselves to be whole and to be happy. But that is a lie. From this day forward, tell yourself that you are enough and repeat it until you start to feel it. Yes, you are "the cake," and you are enough! Go about treating yourself the way you would like to be treated by others. Fill your own cup with love, the way you would for someone you care for.

Would you believe that deep within you is an inner voice calling out not to judge yourself so harshly? When you feel confused or foggy, when you don't know what to do, a loud voice in your head tells you to follow society's expectations. But beneath that voice is the gentle whisper of your intuition, deep within. If you increase its volume, it will help you clean out the cobwebs and lead you to let go of your fears. This is your higher intuitive voice, which underlies your everyday awareness. It will guide you on the journey to explore your gifts, your potential, and your life's possibilities. Be aware, observe in the moment, and listen with the utmost attention of your being. Achieving this is easiest when you are in a state of calm. In a later chapter, you will learn how to meditate and attune yourself to your intuitive voice that lives within your subconscious.

Let me tell you a story of how loving myself changed my perspective, brought on confidence, and helped me radiate love to others. It put me in the realm of happiness. One day, in a wheelchair, I was accompanied by my husband to meet a medical specialist. After carrying out many tests which were non-diagnostic, he speculated out loud that I would one day have a degenerative illness. I listened, and I usually would be sensitive and well up with tears if someone told me something like that. But after many years of practicing and knowing that I am worthy of myself, I answered in a voice that took even me by surprise, "My other doctors suggest that the results are inconclusive. How can you predict that my future may involve a degenerative disease?"

I continued, "I have learned to love myself, and I hope you realize that you are making your patient feel negative and unhappy when there is no data to suggest a diagnosis or such a poor prognosis. Why wouldn't you paint a picture which is not so gloomy, but one with a bit of sunshine when there is this level of uncertainty and such an opportunity for hope?" He looked at me, startled, while the medical resident in the room mumbled below her breath and nodded her head in agreement. The doctor's manner changed in that instant, and he politely took my hand in his and smiled. I am in the best hands now under his guidance and care. Self-love can be so strong and beautiful that it radiates out to the others around you and puts you in a confident, secure, and stable position. Accepting who you are and knowing you are enough is the basis for finding happiness.

This feeling resonates in my heart and mind that I love myself. It is possible to do so much more, experience more, let the doors open with possibilities, once you are honest with yourself and commit to loving yourself. Growing up in my culture, I was taught that a woman can have thoughts and feelings but is expected to be demure and respectful. Respectful meant not voicing your opinions or contradicting anyone. So what did I do? I stuffed my feelings and became more and more unhappy. I did everything I was told to do, but was I being honest with myself? Absolutely not!

Be your own best friend, and respect yourself and the relationship you have with yourself. You are human, and we all fail, make mistakes, and sometimes hurt or do bad things. Young children make mistakes, by dropping a jar of candy, punching their sibling, or pulling the dog's tail, and we teach them to do better, but do we hate them? No, because we know that they have lessons to learn. In the same way, we need to start forgiving our own mistakes and accepting ourselves for who we are. Reach out to yourself with care and love, the way you would treat a child. Stand tall in your own presence, and know that you are enough the way you are. Love yourself with a love not based on gimmicks or rewards, but a love that is pure and always there for you.

Think of your best friend for a moment. Are you there for them in adverse and joyous times? Of course you are! You talk with them and help them when they go through a rough patch and bask with them in their happy times. Now look in a mirror and gaze at yourself, and try to be aware of what you are looking at. Yes, you may have a bad hair day or dark patches under your eyes or wrinkles—or maybe glowing skin and sparkly eyes. Look a bit deeper at your reflection. That is just your outer appearance. Look within and ask yourself, "Is the person I am looking at in the mirror my best friend?" If the answer is no, then here is when I want you to look into your eyes in the mirror and say: "I love myself unconditionally and accept myself for who I am. I will, from this moment on, respect myself, have compassion for myself, empower myself, and trust myself." Say this loudly a few times until you feel an internal shift from the compelling affirmation you are stating. Perhaps you need to say it every morning while brushing your hair until it is an integral part of you. Perhaps you need to write it down in your journal and memorize it.

When you face a difficult situation, be patient and accept yourself, just as you would your best friend. The same goes for when you are celebrating a happy time. Go ahead and be open to trying this. You are on the track of being who indeed you are, and this affirmation will open doors for you, in more ways than one, with the expansive abundance and happiness that awaits you.

A MULTILAYERED CAKE

The baumkuchen cake is famously known as the "king of cakes" in Europe. "Baumkuchen" means "tree cake" in German, on account of its vertical layers, which look like the growth rings of a tree. It is also a dessert in Japan, where it is known as "keeki." The paper-like layers, in a single slice, look like the cross-section of a tree trunk. The cake is cooked on a spit, and when you bite into a slice, you can see and taste each layer.

Self-love is like a baumkuchen cake. Each layer is fragile, but when put together as a whole, the layers hold themselves majestically. We need to build on each individual layer of our personality and bring the sheets together to be one unique entity.

THE LAYER OF SELF-ACCEPTANCE

Are you accepting yourself for who you truly are with all your flaws? Do you hate yourself and get angry that you are not able to be like others? Do you keep comparing yourself? Perhaps you get confused and are filled with envy and jealousy. You forget that you are unique and are loved for who you are. As humans, we are continuously evolving, and if you try to understand that you are "the cake," that you are the essence with all its imperfections and perfections, then you will realize that it is okay to love and accept yourself unconditionally.

Anya was an artist, as was Mel, her friend. Mel had many followers on Twitter and was famous for her art and connections in the art world. She was going to show her work in an art gallery and had invited Anya, who she thought would be a support. But while Anya politely smiled and spoke nicely to Mel, inside she felt deeply jealous that she was not as illustrious in the art field as her friend. She started to loathe herself and feel angrier and more envious. Though Anya had her own unique and beautiful qualities, she could not see them, being caught up in the mind chatter telling her she was not good enough. If Anya had self-acceptance, appreciating and acknowledging herself for who she is instead of judging herself by external standards, she would have been pleased for her friend Mel. She would have known that she herself was worthy, and the opportune time would possibly arise where she would get to shine, too. The only person suffering here was Anya.

We tend to compare ourselves with others when it comes to our appearance, our families, our materialistic assets, and our careers. We search outside ourselves for acceptance and appreciation, but honestly, we have to look within and understand how truly magnificent we are. We hurt ourselves by judging ourselves, causing anger, loathing, and sadness. Work at being your own best friend, and remind yourself of your value by saying, "I am the cake!" Come on, let me hear it! Let me see you stand tall, smile, and repeat it again.

Questions for Your Journal

1. Do you frequently compare yourself with others? Do you feel pressure from others to "be better" than you are? Who causes that feeling in you —peers? family? colleagues? the media? society? What areas of your life does this affect?

2. Do you acknowledge yourself and pat yourself on the back for the way you are holding up or are you starving yourself of appreciation?

THE LAYER OF SELF-FORGIVENESS

It is not easy to forgive yourself if you do not accept yourself. Forgiving ourselves is sometimes hard but necessary. It is a choice we make to let go rather than to hold onto the pain and anguish. Some of us hold onto the feeling that we are wrong and do not understand that forgiving ourselves is essential. The most successful people in the world have failed umpteen times, picked themselves up, and carried on. They are the ones who gather nuggets of information and learning from their lessons of failure and carry them onto another new adventure. They do not let a failure stop them from achieving what they want. Successful people do not blame or shame themselves and tend to be less self-judgmental. Let go and realize that you are only human and that we all make mistakes. Along the way to success, we have many failures, and this is one of the ways we learn and do better.

When you were a young child, you made many a mistake, but there was no sense of worry or failure. You went on your way exploring and doing something new. To let go of our past, we need to forgive ourselves, care for ourselves with compassion and acceptance, and move on. We tend to forget that forgiveness for ourselves is as important as forgiving someone else for their wrongdoing. The more you hold onto the pain of not forgiving yourself, it builds up inside of you and stirs up internal troubles.

Lee was a lovely lady who was disturbed and unhappy with how she had yelled at her daughter Sue, who wanted to go on a vacation with friends. After the quarrel, Lee put on an appearance that all was okay, but inside she felt terrible. She was upset that Sue had chosen her friends to travel with rather than her family. Lee's thoughts kept going to how unfair it was, but she also felt guilt for yelling. She couldn't seem to get past her negative feelings.

Lee spoke with a close friend who gently made her realize that her daughter had come to have an open discussion with her mother. Lee felt even more upset and frustrated that she had belittled her daughter. She apologized to Sue for the way she had behaved. Together they calmly discussed the topic of the vacation, and in the end, they both hugged each other.

Feeling guilty, Lee realized she had to forgive herself for what she had done and put it in the past. That way she could continue to have a happy relationship with her daughter, but most of all, a comfortable relationship with herself. Today Lee is wiser and understands that holding onto the past creates blocks in relationships that make her feel miserable. When she makes a mistake, she realizes that she did the best she could at the time, and forgives herself.

It is okay to say "sorry" to yourself and genuinely mean it, for we all make rash decisions and mistakes. Accept and be kind to yourself for the errors and learn to let go of the past and be in the present. Without forgiving oneself, peace is unreachable.

Recently I had to forgive myself in a big way. It took me time to realize that not forgiving myself was causing pain in a specific part of my body. I never knew that all the strong, negative emotions could lead to hidden changes in our physical and mental state. I practiced the Emotional Free Technique (EFT or "tapping"), which you will learn in one of the later chapters. I realized the root of my problem, accepted myself with love even in the difficult situation, and tapped. After a few rounds of the EFT, I felt the difference, and the pain dissipated as if someone had waved a magic wand.

Questions for Your Journal

1. *Are you critical and judgmental toward yourself, routinely blaming and shaming yourself when you make a mistake? If the answer is yes, how does that attitude serve you? Does it benefit you or others in any way?*

2. *What benefit would there be to you or others if instead you forgave yourself and let go of your mistake?*

3. *What specific mistakes(s) are you blaming yourself for—holding onto— at this very moment?*

4. *Do you realize that you did what you could to the best of your ability at the time? Are you willing to forgive yourself for these errors?*

5. *Make the decision to forgive yourself. Repeat these words out loud, "I love and have compassion for myself. I forgive myself for all my mistakes. I let them go. I have learned from them, and now I move on, a better person and richer in wisdom."*

6. *Write the above affirmation down in your journal and return to it anytime you start to judge yourself.*

THE LAYER OF SELF-COMPASSION

What is self- compassion? It is treating oneself with kindness and understanding, the way you would treat your friend in a situation of difficulty, pain, rejection, or failure.

We tend to treat ourselves with harsh criticism and judgment. Our society instills in us a need to be the best. Whether it be reaching the top tier of management, being admitted to an Ivy League university, or standing out as the most fashionable in a group, we put undue stress and pressure on ourselves. We have been taught to motivate ourselves with self-criticism rather than self-compassion.

If your friend was not selected for a work position, you would offer to listen and not pass judgment. You would be compassionate, understanding that we all have moments of failure. But what if *you* failed to acquire a work position? Would you be understanding? You would likely feel angry, defensive, and crushed, then start beating yourself up.

If instead you treated yourself with some kindness and understanding, you would not feel so lonely and sad at the loss of the promotion. Having a balanced emotional mindset, you would regard your disappointing experience as an opportunity to learn. You would pick yourself up and do better the next time.

I have noticed in our high schools the pressure is very high for the students. They often are taught that getting a high grade is good but not great unless it is the highest grade in the class. The child then incorporates this message into her life and cannot ever fail or have a momentary lapse, as she is expected to excel in all circumstances. It is not enough that she does her personal best: she must be better than everyone around her. This unreasonably competitive attitude imposes self-judgment on a child and causes mental suffering. Instead we should be teaching our kids that life is all about living each day as a gift, with gratitude, and that we should honor ourselves for being who we are.

I know a veterinarian who gives to her animal patients around the clock with compassion and caring. But she was so critical of herself that she felt she was not doing enough to care for the animals. She was unnecessarily hard on herself. Being kind to others is important, but not at the expense of not being compassionate with yourself.

In my yoga class I learned that the sense of touch helps us learn self-compassion. It is beneficial to gently stroke your skin when you are hurt or upset. Nerve signals inform the brain that the stroking is pleasant, and the stroking impulses help to deaden the pain impulses. This is being kind and compassionate toward yourself. Giving a self-hug helps, too.

Self-compassion means being kind to ourselves in times of inadequacy, failure, or suffering. People who are self-compassionate comfort themselves in times of hardship.

We are all, as part of humanity, interlinked. Remembering that personal flaws and suffering are shared by humanity helps us understand that difficulties happen to us all, not just to ourselves individually. We are not being personally targeted.

Being mindful of our negative emotions—observing them without judgment—is a big part of self-compassion. As author Dr. Kristin Neff points out, "We cannot ignore our pain and feel compassion for it at the same time. At the same time, mindfulness requires that we not be 'over-identified' with thoughts and feelings, so that we are caught up and swept away by negative reactivity."

Questions for Your Journal

1. *Jot down a circumstance where you were judging yourself. What was your inner-critic voice saying? How did it make you feel?*

2. *Now write down what your inner voice would have been saying if you had practiced self-compassion in that situation. How would that have made you feel?*

3. *Write down this sentence in your journal three times: "I choose the power of compassion, and I am worth it." Next time you start criticizing yourself, be aware of what you are doing, and stop. Instead, repeat that sentence aloud three times, with feeling. Treat yourself as you would treat a friend. Be kind and understanding of yourself!*

THE LAYER OF SELF-TRUST

Build trust by listening to your inner voice and intuition. To believe in yourself is to respect your own opinions and not be swayed by other people's viewpoints. To be confident, make your choices and set your mind to do anything you decide to do.

Lily always doubted herself and agreed to everything other people said. She did not like to confront or have her opinion out there. Lily lacked confidence and had the habit of stuffing her thoughts down and causing internal grief, which kept playing out in different situations in her life. One day she was speaking to her mother-in-law, who took her for someone who would never speak up or confront her. Lily spoke gently but at the same time in a confident voice: "I don't like how you take all the credit and tell everyone that you are the one who organized the party for everyone!" Lily at first did not realize she had said this and, shocked at herself, wondered, "What did I do?" Then she felt a warm rush of blood through her body along with a tingling sensation, telling her that this was what she truly had wanted to say, and it was time now to trust herself and speak up. Her mother-in-law was also taken aback. She hemmed and hawed and tried to change the subject. Lily was proud of herself and felt the self-love. It felt great not to be doubting herself. She had taken a stand for her own self-worth and was never troubled again by her mother-in-law. They actually came to treat each other with mutual respect.

The quicker we learn to trust ourselves, the faster we can start living life, release suffering, and move toward happiness. Make slow changes and shifts toward believing in yourself, and have tolerance and patience through this journey.

Self-esteem and self-trust go hand-in-hand. Self-esteem is genuine trust in who you are and what you can achieve. You are able to be confident and move forward with who you are. To have good self-esteem, you must feel that you can do your best and make progress toward your goals. You must feel good about yourself and be able to express your thoughts, opinions, and values truthfully. Self-trust is letting that inner voice or true essence within guide you. It's knowing that you are on the right path, with no need to be judged by societal expectations or your unkind inner voice.

I went through a rough spell earlier in my life when I moved to a neighborhood filled with high crime. Due to that and to my visa status, I was unable to work. The area I lived in was unsafe for walking, so I was cooped up at home without a computer, radio, and television. Dire financial circumstances brought on more hardships, where I did not have the money to call and speak internationally with my parents and friends. I was lonely and had no opportunity to do what I wanted. Over time I lost my feeling of self-worth, confidence, and my will to succeed. I began to change from having a sunny disposition to a person who felt lost and with no purpose. A couple of years later, I was able to move out of that area and came to a sunny city—a city where I could walk without fear of being mugged. I enrolled in a few classes and slowly but surely started to believe in myself. I gradually regained my confidence and my will to live life with positivity and happiness. I trusted and felt true to myself. I felt the light shine within me, the feeling of sheer delight and gratitude to be living this wondrous life. Looking back, I realize this was a tremendous learning experience in which I gathered knowledge along the way.

Everyone is talented at something. We all have unique abilities with which we can shine. Our talents give us reason to trust ourselves and using them in the service of others gives us self-esteem. For instance, my husband is very good at using technology and also at working with his hands. He has a golden heart and likes to assist people in these ways. Working with computers and smartphones, wiring sound systems, and fixing cars are his special gifts. Knowing this builds his self-confidence, and he feels pleased and satisfied knowing that he is helping people.

Eva likes to create meals and learn new ways of making appetizers and entrees. Her talent is to please friends through the stomach with good food. Taking this further, she has organizational skills and is often requested by friends and groups to assist them in making an event fun with her umpteen ideas and dishes. She recognizes her talents and has built her self-esteem and internal comfort with this.

Self-esteem is based on love for yourself and knowing that you can be the best in any situation and feel good about yourself.

Questions for Your Journal

1. *Do you take time to be quiet inside and listen to your inner voice with trust? Or do you easily get swayed by others and find yourself making rash decisions?*

2. *Do you get caught up in overanalyzing on account of self-distrust and anxiety?*

3. *Do you put off making important decisions because of self-doubt?*

4. *Jot down a list of your strengths. Are you talented at something? Write down what you think you are good at along with your good qualities. We all have a unique gift given to us to explore and use. After writing down all the things you are good at, does that help you pinpoint your unique talent? If so, what is it?*

5. *Repeat this statement a few times: "I respect and value myself for the gifts given to me and for who I am."*

THE LAYER OF SELF-RESPECT

Self-respect is listening to your core values and making choices with dignity and integrity. If you deviate from your values with your actions, then you are not true to yourself and tend to lose self-respect. It's important to have a steadfast dedication to making decisions that favor you.

For example, if you are in an unhealthy relationship and let someone treat you in a degrading way, that could easily damage your self-respect. In our changing modern society, we sometimes feel lonely and unsupported. That can tempt us to settle for any sort of relationship. We try to fill the gaps with any kind of love. We do not realize that first and foremost we need to feel the love for ourselves.

Atrocious stories have cropped up of women who immigrated from other countries and have stayed in their marriage regardless of being physically abused. They are frowned upon by people from the home who espouse the home country's cultural values. To protect their parents from being ostracized by their community, the women stay in these abusive relationships, as they cannot return to their parent's home. In such extreme, bleak cases, it does take courage and all the love you have for yourself to realize that you need to break this complicated pattern by reaching out to a friend, emotional mentor, support group, or organization dealing with these complex issues.

Having self- respect is when you care for and honor your mind and body. You learn to acknowledge that you have a voice and that you must stand up and face your difficult situations. When flying on planes, we are advised to first place the oxygen mask on ourselves before assisting others in times of emergency. In the same way, we must first love and respect ourselves, and care for ourselves, before we can effectively be of use to others in the totally loving way we wish to be. By taking care of ourselves first, we are able to give others the love and help they deserve.

Do you stuff your emotions rather than expressing them and standing up for yourself? Do you feel you must apologize for being emotional?

When people make fun of you, do you pretend you don't feel hurt and join in the laughter, making light of the ridicule? Do you look at your body and say, "I am ugly?" Do you tell yourself you are not smart enough? If you said yes to any of these questions, then let's work on building up the terrific respect you should have for yourself. No one should put you down or make you feel demoralized. That behavior is not acceptable! Say it loudly, for you to hear and accept: "I am the cake!" Say it until you feel the words seep into every part of your being as truth. You must practice changing your thoughts and beliefs to those that provide you with self-esteem, respect, acknowledgment, appreciation, love, and forgiveness. That's what you will learn to do in this book.

Mia was a lovely young girl who was dominated by her siblings and parents. She felt she was an unworthy person. She had tried at various times to stop the siblings from teasing her. Mia felt no one listened to her. She wanted to convey her ideas in family discussions. One day she threw a tantrum. She could hear her inner voice tell her that she couldn't accept any more of this. She told her family to stop their behavior and then in a gentler tone explained why. Her family stood still and in shock, but they were attentive and eager to learn what was causing the unhappiness in their dear Mia. She explained that all she was asking was not to be teased anymore and to be heard during discussions. Then she would feel valued and more a part of the family. Mia's welling up of self-respect was perceived by her family and gave them a new respect for her. From then on, they no longer teased her and made an effort to have Mia participate in their discussions.

Take charge of your life and who you are. Self-respect will flower in you when you make the decision to do this!

35

THE LAYER OF SELF-EMPOWERMENT

Self-empowerment is the feeling you have when you act and move toward a goal regardless of others' judgment or approval. We have our own power and our own conscience and do not need recognition from others.

Bob came home smiling after work, and his wife wondered why he was so energized and happy. It had been a difficult few months of workplace politics, trying to convince his skeptical bosses and other management teams to see and accept his idea. Bob had a vision of a way to build their product in a more efficient way. He had been hounded with questions and doubted by the senior management, but he kept following his plan, communicating, and trying to work with everyone. And this had been the day when all his concerted efforts paid off. His idea was accepted by the bosses and board members, too. He felt a rush of tingling happiness move through his body, releasing his tension and anxiety. He felt pride and accomplishment that his idea had finally been taken seriously. His perseverance— staying true to his vision and patiently promoting it—resulted in success and a marvelous feeling of self-empowerment.

Jana was part of a group of friends she felt she could not leave. She did not fit in, as they were gossip-mongers and made her feel unhappy. But Jana longed for their acceptance and recognition. She was scared to tell them how she felt, as she feared being alone. What actually was going on with Jana? Fear and uncertainty had confused her, and she thought she could not stand on her own. She didn't know that she had the power to trust her own inner guidance and that she could overcome her fear. Many of us have gone through this feeling of needing the wrong kind of love just to feel wanted. Jana needed to take her power back to feel good again. She slowly distanced herself from the group and kept repeating positive affirmations. Over time she found a group of friends who respected her and made her feel wanted. She came to feel empowered and good about herself.

Listen to your own voice. Don't get swayed by the noise of the world. We each have a knowing, a guiding voice, deep within us. Once you know that, you can make your own choices and act upon them. Let go of the expectations, stereotypes, and roles formed for you by society and the media. Move toward the true you, which will lead you in the direction of happiness. Make the shift now toward empowering yourself!

Questions for Your Journal

1. *Do you feel powerless or do you take responsibility for your life and your decisions?*

2. *Do you worry about what other people think? Do you listen to your inner voice when you need to decide what to do, or do other people's advice and opinions guide you through life?*

3. *Close your eyes, take some deep breaths, and sit silently for a few minutes. Then think of a problem that has been bothering you or a situation that's confusing you. Ask your inner guidance what the right solution is. Then sit silently and simply listen. Chances are a feeling or thought will come up that directs you to a new way of regarding the issue. Or an insight may come later in the day, or as you are falling asleep. Perhaps you will wake up in the morning just knowing the answer. After you try this technique, write in your journal about what you experienced.*

Chapter 3

Restocking the Kitchen

To bake beautiful cakes and cook up wonderful food, you need to clear out unhealthy and expired foods and replace them with healthier choices. To create the joyful experiences we want, we need to let go of disempowering habits and replace them with new ones.

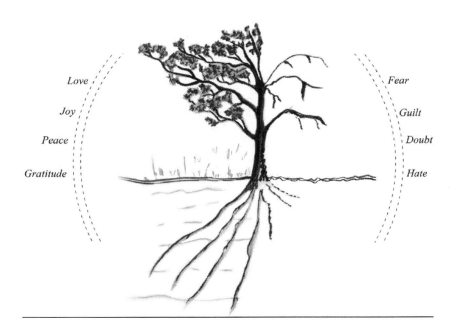

Let's leave the baking analogy for a moment and consider the metaphor of a tree. Picture a tree where on one side the branches are dried-up and brittle, without any leaves or blossoms. You can see the bare roots uncovered and exposed to the blistering sun. The branches represent fear, guilt, doubt, and hate. On the other side of the tree, imagine branches that are healthy and sturdy with green leaves, blossoming flowers, and the roots covered in fertile, moist soil. These branches represent love, joy, peace, and gratitude.

Most of us have both kinds of branches in our lives, but in our hearts we want to get rid of the old, dead wood and be a tree that displays on all sides luscious leaves, beautiful blossoms, and fragrant aroma, with a robust trunk and branches reaching outward toward the sky, with roots anchored down into the earth, stable and balanced. To be that tree, we must master the negative feelings of fear, guilt, doubt, and hate, letting the branches break off and replacing them with the new life of expanding love, joy, peace, and gratitude. Above all, we must pursue self-love, so important in generating the positive feelings which we so richly deserve.

I have experienced my share of difficult times, but through accepting who I am and loving myself, I have learned to replace the bad with the good, unlocking the hidden beauty within me. This has led me to an expansive and abundant life. Let's explore further and the techniques a person can use to calm the mind and body and experience the feeling of bliss.

LETTING GO OF PERFECTIONISM

There is a difference between being a perfectionist and being a high achiever. A high achiever sets goals that are reachable and attainable. A perfectionist has goals that are unrealistic and unattainable, setting unfair standards for herself and others.

A perfectionist wants to excel but is strict and inflexible. She thinks of how others will judge or view her and her actions. Wanting to be so perfect, sometimes she procrastinates. The inner judgmental voice continuously pounds away, creating thoughts that make her feel she is not worthy or good enough. This may lead to anxiety and fear. The perfectionist is overcome with fear that if she starts a task, she may not do it perfectly enough. She may be unable even to take the first step in starting a project, being so concerned that that first step must be 100% accurate. This is different from the procrastinator who is lazy and puts off work for a very different reason.

Rita walked in proudly to show her parents her final grades. She sat on the couch with a smile on her face. She looked up at her mother, who was scowling. Rita had done exceptionally well in all her subjects and had aced many of her classes, but her mother kept staring at the report card, and then she turned her harsh gaze on her daughter. Rita froze and felt her mother's displeasure go through her like a cold, Alaskan wind. She had a 'B' in her foreign language class, and her mother could not accept this. The mom's strong disapproval continued over the years. Rita was always inclined to be a perfectionist, especially in the learning field. She had internalized her mother's critical voice, telling her to do it this way or no way. An unappreciative parent can instill perfectionist ways in a child that become more severe over time. This can cause great unhappiness and loss of self-esteem.

If you are a perfectionist, here are some things you can do to reduce that tendency and start enjoying your life:

- Understand the root cause of your perfectionism, to reduce the heavy judgment and criticism toward yourself. Who or what caused you to develop perfectionist tendencies?

- Be aware that you're a perfectionist. Hear the critic's voice inside you and acknowledge that it exists.

- Tell this voice to subside a bit, and let in a new and gentler voice, the guiding voice of your creative intuition.

- Find a different way to proceed in starting and carrying out your tasks. Approach a task as something fun that you can enjoy, rather than do it just to check it off your list. Smell the roses along the way! Enjoy the process!

- Welcome the new, less perfectionistic you. Be gentle and compassionate with yourself, and when you make mistakes, forgive yourself and let go of the doubt, anxiety, and fear.

Questions for Your Journal

1. *Do you hear a judgmental inner voice directing your every move? Does it direct just one area of your life or several, or does it direct them all? Which areas does this critical voice affect?*

2. *Do you feel you are judged by others? Do you do things on account of what they think and want rather than because you want to? Do you want to be acknowledged every step of the way by others?*

3. *Do you set unattainable, unrealistic goals for yourself and others? Do you understand the difference between doing your best and expecting perfection?*

4. *How would your life be different if you became more forgiving of mistakes?*

LETTING GO OF FEAR AND DOUBT

When we let go of fear and doubt, a myriad of possibilities opens up to us. You attract what you keep thinking off. Start to focus on what you want. Do not dwell on what you don't want!

When we fear a loss of something, we set ourselves up to experience the very thing that we don't want to happen. Focus on what you have now, at this moment, and appreciate that. This moment is all that exists. Do not project your thoughts on what you may lose, as that tends to attract what you fear.

Amy felt scared every time she was with Kim, her daughter-in-law. Amy was afraid that Kim would be possessive of her son and that she, Amy, would lose his affection. Fortunately, Amy understood over time that her fears were creating tension between herself and Kim and that if she kept focusing on what she was afraid of, she was likely to bring it about. Kim was not by nature possessive, and Amy at last realized that. Both women became comfortable and happy with each other and developed a positive relationship.

Fear and doubt start eating into a person like poison, and they do not let us live our truth. Fear takes control of us and makes us want to run from it instead of facing it head-on. When you feel afraid, sit in a safe spot and take in a deep breath. Exhale and steady your breathing. Your mind is telling you to run away and not deal with the fear, or to forget about the concern and in its place make excuses. Become aware of your fear and try to determine its root and why the fear is so paralyzing. Know that when you fear, you are being asked to work on improving yourself.
Fear tends to take over our thoughts. Fear attracts more fear, while positive thoughts draw more good thoughts and stimulate positive action.

When we are afraid, a part of the body typically gets knotted up or tightened, or we may feel some other disagreeable sensation. Be patient and kind with yourself, knowing that the fear is causing the discomfort. Identify the dominant thought that is causing it. Take your mind to the spot in your body where the pain or discomfort is.

Place your hand on the spot, inhale, and visualize that the breath is being sent to that spot. Hold your breath for a second or two and release, imagining the discomfort leaving your body with the exhalation. Do this several times until the pain or discomfort is gone. Visualize good, clean air-breath being sent to the tense area as you do this exercise.

We face our fear and make peace with it by becoming aware of it, understanding its root, going into the unknown territory and making the shift, letting go of those automatic thoughts ingrained in us which show up as fear.

Fear has different stages. The most difficult one, where we often get stuck, is the stage of being the victim. The victim feels that someone else or something outside of themselves has put up a roadblock to prevent them from moving forward. When they become aware and take responsibility for themselves, they start to shift, to make an internal change. It is possible to turn the dastardly fear into a powerful emotion of enthusiasm and energy. Later I will show you how to do that.

You will be learning spiritual techniques and ways to unfold your soul, which whispers to you the truth of your gifts, which are locked within you. These techniques will carry you to a world beyond what you have experienced, and the process will be one of joy while achieving your goal. You will learn how to manifest yourself and look beyond your parameters, and how to experience beyond your powers of thinking. You will encounter a paradigm of wonder and knowledge, that leads to the kind of living that each one of us deserves to experience. In the chapters ahead, you will learn how to manifest yourself using different techniques such as affirmations, visualization, meditation, and tapping (the Emotional Freedom Technique). These have played an essential part in my life in unlocking the treasures within me, and I am excited to share them with you.

Life has been mysterious for me, and through the years of ups and downs I gathered learning experiences I talk about in this book. If I had known better, I would have cherished life with open arms. Let me tell you a true story about myself. I took walking for granted until it was taken away from me. Over some months, I could feel my body losing stamina. I was not up to doing my daily activities. It felt like a big boulder had rolled over onto me, and I experienced one of the worst crashes I ever had since becoming chronically ill. I sat and sat on the couch, having no inclination to do anything. Weeks and then months went by, and I sat gazing into the distance, weak and fearful. Was this ever going to change? Was I going back to being bedridden, with no hope of ever walking again? This monstrous fear ate away at me, and I felt weaker and sicker as the days went by. I was stuck in a miserable, unyielding state, and I was being the victim. I could feel a simmering anger start to surface as I got more frustrated and felt more lost and scared. Anger for being in this situation, anger for not wanting to fight this, anger at everything in the world. Lost in my negative thoughts, I felt remorse and fury.

What had happened to me? I used to listen to my soul with its soft, guiding voice. Where was the higher version of me, and why was I not giving myself the chance to listen to the whispers of my intuitive self? Then right in front of my eyes, a vision unfolded. I saw this magical, tiny hummingbird, in all its beauty, drinking the sweet nectar of a bright-red flower. The bird danced in the twilight, to and fro, its wings moving faster than the eye could see, happy in its wondrous enjoyment of life. There was something in me which started to awaken to this glorious sight. If the hummingbird was delighting in life with such joy, couldn't I let go of my anger and fear and be the hummingbird in my life?

I felt this gentle voice guide me from within. It held me with a hug and love and put me on the path of awakening. In an instant, the anger melted in front of my eyes, I knew that I could start loving myself again and accept the circumstances. I let go of the unbridled rage in my body, and welcomed in the feeling of calm, love, and utmost gratitude. Then I told myself, "I am not afraid of anything I have to face. I am me. I accept me the way I am and know that I am well. This feeling is now embedded in me, and I am a changed person, empowered and living in a state of joy and love. Grief and anger have turned into grace and bliss. I am not going to let gnawing fear, hate, anger, or other negative emotions get the better of me. I accept them and observe them at the moment they are there and let them pass. I choose life without the need for pain and suffering."

As I lay down on the couch, I could feel a warm light of love and energy pass through me. I was like a vessel through which the energy of love and peace flowed. The only way I could explain what had just happened was that I felt the presence of the God, or some might call it "divine grace."

I had shifted, and life was open for me to be a part of again, with its wonder and abundance. What do I mean by shifting? Through the intense years of pain, struggle, and anguish, there was now a transformation of consciousness whereby the past and future did not play a role in my identity. With the more profound understanding of my inner being and living for the present moment, I became a happier person. I now feel peace with my inner and outer self. I am truly me, in harmony with my soul, with no ego ripples or negative mind chatter. My fears have dissipated and subsided. I had not been aware that life has always been abundant and wondrous until I went through these upheavals, and it took me a long time to realize that we have to want to live in this better way. Now that I do, life is magical and incredible.

I want to share something more with you. Weeks passed by, and my friends and family helped me with my necessary chores while I rested on the couch, being enveloped with a sense of peace. I listened to the birds, saw the light change, felt the fresh, nippy air change, and I lay there with loving kindness and compassion for myself. One morning, I felt more energy while sitting on the couch and began meditating. It was a gratifying experience of stillness and being in the now. I could hear the whisper in my head grow in clarity, as though speaking to me, and I listened. It was my voice of reason from deep in my subconscious telling me that I was to use my intended gift of giving. Giving to what and to whom? I felt it at that moment that I was being told to expand on my knowledge given to me and share it. Then I came back a split-second later to the mind chaos and normalcy of life.

But I was a changed person after that. I was *the opening* through which life flows. I am now receptive, willing, and filled with feelings of peace, joy, gratitude, and flourishing love for myself and the universe. That doesn't mean that everything is hunky-dory all the time. It means that I look at situations and circumstances in a different light and allow life to flow through me, rather than creating roadblocks.

I went on from there to accumulate different techniques, which furthered my experience of the beauty of life. I pick one or more from my treasure box every day. Today I chose the beautiful pearl and diamond bracelet, the matching earrings, and the simple string of pearls. These represent the techniques I may use such as visualization, meditation, or affirmation. I kept picturing myself with optimal health and in this way manifested what I wanted. Now, after months, I am again able to walk, talk, and even drive. There was no miraculous, sudden change but a slight and steady improvement. I am at peace with myself, and the fear is disarmed.

I am genuinely the better version of myself, reducing my fears, anger, hate, guilt, and envy, letting go of my many attachments and lowering my expectations. I look at life with a sense of serenity and joy and being in the present moment.

I wrote this book for you, so you may have a chance to experience your hidden talent or gift and to help you shift to a paradigm of happiness and peace. Know that you have been blessed, and that it is you who has to make the shift to stand tall in your inner and outer beauty.

Take away its chance, and fear slowly loses it power and the impact it makes on your mind. Enlarge the part of the image, the positive outcome in the foreground, and focus on that instead.

Questions for Your Journal

1. What are you really afraid of?

2. Can you handle the fear and face it now, or will you ignore it and let it keep recurring?

3. If you need help, can you reach out to someone who has gone through something similar? Who would that person be?

4. Can you find a mentor or someone sympathetic for emotional support? Who would that person be?

5. Can you take a step forward and break the fear by focusing on the positive outcome you desire? Write down what that positive outcome is.

6. Can you break the fear into smaller, less frightening parts? What is the worst that can happen?

7. If the fear is not of something that can truly hurt you, picture a place that makes you happy, place the fear in the background, and keep shrinking it to being tiny and farther in the distance. In your journal, write about your experience with this exercise.

LETTING GO OF ANGER AND HATE

Anger is relentless and detrimental. It causes hate and loathing, and puts you in a position of misery. It is like the fiery breath of a monster. It burns slowly within and erupts in an uncontrollable rage, or it may be a deep-seated, intense heat that seethes within us unseen.

Anger can be beneficial in certain stress situations when you release it in a safe environment. If we release it healthily, it can help us act, be creative, and feel empowered. But chronic, unbridled, unchecked anger is harmful and deters our chance for happiness. Repressed and seething anger can be detrimental to our cardiovascular health, blood pressure, and health in general. Chronic anger leads to hurtful and harmful situations which can turn into violent acts. We are unable to stifle this emotion beyond a certain point, and sometimes it releases with so much hate that it causes us and others harm. It is like a volcano erupting with its heat and magma flow, causing havoc and destroying nature and houses in its path.

Anger can reach levels where you have no chance of experiencing even a bit of happiness or peace. Everything around you feels wrong and unproductive, and people start distancing themselves from you. This fierce anger you hold within is displayed via your posture, attitude, and tone of voice. It rips apart your joy and that of others around you.

Learn to let it go off this destructive anger, and you will find a sense of calm come over you. Your thoughts will be more productive, and you will understand what it is to be free from hurting yourself and others.

Sally worked in a technology firm and dealt with many coworkers (and her boss) of the opposite sex. At team and board meetings, she was not taken seriously as a valued member. Sally came home dejected and angry with herself, unable to understand why her opinion was not considered. She made excuses at first to stay away from work, and when she did go in, she snapped at her boss, was rude to the cafeteria lady, and came home with a headache. What was happening to her? The anger and hate started to build within and were destroying her chance to

49

communicate effectively in a diplomatic way. While presenting her project, Sally's voice began to get louder over time. Soon she was choked with emotions but continued with her presentation. Jim, her boss, advised her to take a few days of vacation and rest but did not address why.

Sally could feel a gnawing and rebellious heat within her, and she had to find a way to release it. She remembered how her mother had spoken about ways that she used to release her anger. Simple methods of finding a passion or hobby, exercising, training your brain to know that you are a good person and that it's okay to be happy. She remembered her mother's voice, saying, "Sally, remember you are a beautiful girl. Don't lose sight of that, and always believe in yourself. Be dignified, loving, and kind to yourself and others." Sally did leave that job as she was not able to face her boss or coworkers at that time. She learned to believe in herself more, grew more confident, and slowly the anger disappeared. She learned to love herself and became a much happier person.

Anger can spiral out of control. It can be a powerful way to express yourself, but you must be aware and in control of this emotion. It is essential that it not strike out and become harmful or violent in its expression.

In the following chapters, you will learn many ways to release the monster of harmful anger and replace it with love, peace, joy, and gratitude. You will learn to be angry in a healthy way and become aware when anger is rising and getting out of control so that it does not become aggressive and harmful.

Questions for Your Journal

1. *What are you angry about? Are you angry with yourself or mad at someone or something?*

2. *Do you get so caught up in the emotion of anger that you cannot communicate with others diplomatically, but come off as attacking or defensive? When this happens, how does that make you feel?*

3. *Knowing what you know so far, what can you do to change the emotion of anger, which takes over your clarity of thought?*

LETTING GO OF GUILT

The feeling of guilt occurs when we feel—correctly or incorrectly— that we have done wrong, violating our own moral standards or those of society. Guilt is a universal emotion that we all experience at some time in life.

Iris works fulltime, cares for two teenage children, is married to a working, ambitious man, and has elderly parents. She is part of the "sandwich generation" that cares for the younger, the older, and themselves at the same time. Iris feels pulled in different directions as she juggles her responsibilities to all the people she cares for. She often unfairly judges herself for not doing better. Being unable to give each person the amount of quality time and undivided attention she would like to give, enhances her feeling of guilt. She feels she should be able to please her kids, complete her work, support her husband, and help her aging parents, all at the same time.

Guilt can be healthy or unhealthy. It is a complicated emotion that can be useful or cause harm. Healthy guilt is justified guilt. It can help us move in the direction of morality and ethics. Our society has defined boundaries which guide us not to hurt others and help us achieve our goals. From a young age, we are taught that our hurtful actions will have consequences, that to live in a civilized society we need to adhere to certain rules and behave accordingly. A feeling of guilt is instilled in us, and when we do something wrong, that emotion helps us realize it. But holding onto justified guilt is a mistake. It's important, rather, to admit our mistake, apologize for it, make restitution, and move on. We should learn from the mistake, do our best to fix it, then let it go. Holding onto justified guilt turns it into unhealthy guilt, that causes harm both to us and others.

Neil was crying in his third-grade classroom, and the teacher asked if he was okay. He felt terrible that he had punched his friend Lee on the playground. His emotional expression of guilt signified something was wrong. Neil told the teacher he wanted to go apologize to Lee. If Neil had not been taught that punching friends was wrong, he would not have felt the emotion of guilt. But he had been taught well by his parents and had a conscience. For him to grow emotionally, it was important for him to be aware of the wrongness of his act and the consequences of hurting his friend's feelings, and to apologize. But afterwards, Neil would have to let go of his guilty feeling and try to establish a better relationship with Lee. It was beneficial in this circumstance for Neil to experience guilt and feel remorse. Guilt helped him learn from his error so he could change his ways in the future.

Unhealthy guilt occurs when we hold onto the guilt instead of making restitution, then letting the incident go, and moving on. Unhealthy guilt can also occur when we feel responsible for something bad that we are not responsible for. For instance, people often feel it is their fault when someone they dearly love passes away. They may lament, "If only I had insisted he go to the doctor sooner, he would still be with us today." Unhealthy guilt like this is crippling. The person unfairly blames himself for something he had no control over, or for something he would have done differently if he knew back then what he knows today. Unhealthy guilt fills us up with hating ourselves, lowers our self-esteem, and leads to depression. Our ability to help others is also impaired, as our attention is on our sorrow rather than on the present moment and the good we can do in the now. This unhinging guilt informs us that we are wrong when we haven't done anything wrong.

If we have not processed our guilt, worked through it, and moved on, we tend to hide it deeply within us, not wanting to confront the emotion. The guilt lies dormant, like a fuse ready to explode. It can erupt like a volcano, raining lava and rock, destroying our sanity and health, and robbing us of our dreams.

Kate was asked by her mother to pick up groceries, cook a meal, clean the house, and run some errands, as their large family had been invited over for dinner. Kate had planned to get the groceries, but her mother was now asking her to do so much more. She didn't have the time as she had previous commitments. But instead of communicating this to her mother, Kate felt guilty and kept her thoughts to herself. She told herself she was useless and never helped her mother enough, which is what she was often told by her mother. Kate believed she was selfish not to do what was asked of her. She should please her mother and family. This guilt replayed in her mind, but she was unaware that it was causing her unhappiness and that it came up in many areas of her life. It was a repeated pattern. Kate shopped for the groceries, cleaned the house, and cooked most of the meal, but she was very disturbed within. This nagging feeling of guilt was playing havoc with her emotions.

If Kate knew more about "I am the cake," she would have realized she deserved to be happy and confident. She would know that she is magnificent and should be kind to herself. Kate did not deliberately want to hurt her mother or family members. She thought she should be responsible for her mother's hurt feelings. Kate needed to gently speak up and voice her opinion and ask for some help, rather than stuffing her feelings and experiencing unjustified guilt.

We are responsible for our feelings and not responsible for others' feelings unless we have intentionally harmed or hurt them. Let go of that critical voice and the nagging feeling of guilt. Learn to communicate your needs with diplomacy. Let go of the need to be judged as favorable by others and to please others at all time. Be who you truly are and respect yourself.

Unhealthy guilt disrupts our equilibrium and peace and instead brings feelings of blame, hate, anger, and resentment. This kind of guilt may stem from an abusive childhood, a traumatic event, or an illness. There is a root to the deflating guilt that leads to a sense of unworthiness and violates our chance to live happily. We must figure out the root cause of the feeling and honestly examine if the guilt is justified. If it is, we need to make reparation. If it is not, we need to let it go. We need to treat ourselves with loving kindness in these circumstances. We need to forgive ourselves to release the guilt and to move in a positive direction.

We can get stuck in a vicious cycle of guilt and need to break the pattern. A pattern can be observed in different scenarios, such as with our peer group, in our workplace, and with our family. It boils down to letting go, forgiving yourself with compassion, and changing the detrimental habit of self-blame. Be in the moment, let go of the past, and make the shift to start loving yourself. In this way you can release the anger, resentment, and the hold of the gnawing, unhealthy guilt and move to a place of peace and love.

Accept yourself, understand that guilt has taken you by its claws, unclench and release by the act of self-forgiveness. When you let go of unhealthy guilt, you are not trapped anymore in the dark dungeon of blame, shame, and fear.

Remember that we all are imperfect and must learn to accept ourselves and the mistakes we make. Apologize to yourself and then make the necessary changes. The act is done, and you have forgiven yourself.

Know that you can forgive others once you learn to forgive yourself. Give yourself the precious gift of self-forgiveness, and you will be on your way to loving yourself.

Questions for Your Journal

1. *What do you feel guilty about? Is this healthy guilt or unhealthy guilt?*

2. *How much does guilt dominate your awareness? Do you only feel it occasionally, or has it taken over your life?*

3. *What causes you to feel guilty? Is it your conscience? Or is it unreasonable norms and standards imposed by others, such as family, peers, or the media?*

4. *Think of a time when you forgave yourself and another time when you forgave someone else. What were the beautiful emotions that you experienced?*

5. *If you have unhealthy guilt, write down or say out loud what you feel guilty for and that you unconditionally forgive yourself. Repeat the words until you feel you believe them. If the guilty feeling arises in you again, respond to it by repeating that you unconditionally love and forgive yourself.*

FILLING UP WITH LOVE, PEACE, GRATITUDE, AND WELL-BEING

In this chapter we have seen how anger, guilt, fear, doubt, and hate are emotions that impair and limit our lives, in the same way clutter impairs our ability to move about and make wonderful food in the kitchen. To create a wonderful life, we need to let go of the negative and invite the good and positive to take its place. Once our negative emotions release their hold on us, we can fill up with love, peace, gratitude, and well-being. We start to feel empowered with the love and understanding we show ourselves.

Each and every cake is unique, with all its ingredients well-stirred and blended. The integration of love, gratitude, and joy makes us stand in our own beauty.

We all want to be happy, and we are the ones who have to take responsibility for our happiness. Happiness doesn't magically appear in front of you; you have to want it and look deep within yourself, knowing that it is yours. Finding love for yourself, being grateful for what you have, being in the moment, living with a sense of well-being and peace, brings us the feeling of happiness.

It is a state which we all want to attain, but to have it, we must be patient, determined, and compassionate with ourselves. We must learn to change our thoughts. We must let go of the past and not get caught up worrying about what will unfurl in our future. We should try to reduce our expectations of ourselves and others. Deep within us, there is a well-spring of happiness. Explore and find it. Rejoice in it, for this is your inmost nature.

Life for me has included times of beauty and of adversity. I still go through bouts of my illness from time to time. I know that only way to start getting better is to focus on happy thoughts. I don't take things for granted, and I thank my body, mind, spirit, and soul for the smallest of things. I live in the moment. It may be a tough one. If it is, I observe it and let it pass through me, and then I am in the next moment. I have stopped blaming others or asking why I am going through a rough patch. The past no longer has a hold on me. Instead, I learn from the lessons of life and move on. The negative self- talk and chaotic mind-racing is reduced by meditating and tapping daily. Life is mine for choosing how I want to live. I am grateful and filled with love and thank the universe and divine grace for showing me what happiness is.

Are you always waiting for that moment when you think you will be happy? Maybe you think it will be when you finish that project or get that promotion, or when you find the right partner and get married, or when you make your first million. The truth is, you never become happy in some future time, because the future is never here; it's always something you're waiting for. Happiness only happens in the now. It awakens in us when we find peace in the moment. Don't make any more excuses for why you can't be happy right now. That only sabotages your chance for happiness. Let go of the past and future, and be in the present moment.

I mentioned that we need to fill up with love. Love is respect, compassion, trust, forgiveness, acceptance, a feeling of worthiness and understanding. It's a sense of knowing and responsibility that you are magnificent and unique. Say it as many times as you need to, loudly: "I am the cake!" Love is finding the happiness within, finding it around you in people, nature, or in any other way by finding the splendor of what you have been given.

Love is strength and courage in being and accepting yourself for who you are. The more you feel the love for yourself, the more you will displace the feelings of anger, hate, fear, doubt, and guilt and in their place assimilate the spirit of gratitude. You will understand that love permeates all that you are and do. Feel the magic of love, and do not be afraid to show your love out of fear of social pressure or because earlier life teachings have molded you into something that is false. Make the changes, and be *you*!

I talked about filling up with gratitude. Gratitude is an attitude that has to be cultivated and learned. It must be developed as a personality trait that brings about emotional maturity.

Thank-you for the ooey-gooey sludge

In our fast-paced, consumer society, do we have time for the emotion of gratitude? We are always trying to reach a goal, and when we achieve it, we strive for the next one without taking time to appreciate our success. Stop and celebrate the small victories along the road of life. Gratitude will ease the difficult times you face by helping you remember how fortunate you are. Take a moment and think about what you are grateful for, such as the love of your family or friends or the beauty of nature. What about being grateful just for being you? When you live in the soft emotion of gratitude, you find that your fears and doubts disappear, and you feel blessed with the wonders in your midst.

Being grateful is beneficial to our well-being and happiness. Showing appreciation and acknowledging another person can help build stronger relationships, whether with your spouse, children, parents, in-laws, work colleagues, or new acquaintances.

Scientific research suggests that gratitude improves both mental and physical health. It increases happiness and decreases anger and sadness. Being grateful improves our self-esteem. You do not have to compare yourself to another person. Gratitude leads to a feeling of self-confidence and less envy and jealousy.

Raj was troubled and anxious at hearing that his child had been in an accident and that her car had been destroyed. His body shook with fear, but when he reached the hospital and saw his daughter with a slight gash on her forehead and a fractured arm, he started weeping. He told his daughter how grateful he was that the paramedics had taken her to the hospital so swiftly. He also felt gratitude toward the nurses and doctors for taking such good care of his precious girl. Raj knew in his heart, and voiced it aloud, that he was the most fortunate and appreciative man to have his daughter alive and well. He penned a thank-you note to the medical staff and to the paramedics, showing his appreciation. Thanking them helped Raj heal emotionally in such a traumatic time. Being grateful helped foster resilience. Raj had learned to look for the good in any situation and to appreciate the smallest of things in his life. He found this made him more at ease and happier.

How do you cultivate a resilient, strong attitude of gratitude? Here are some suggestions:

1. Keep a gratitude journal, where each day you list three things you are thankful for. Alternatively, each day voice aloud three things. It's fine to list even very small things, such as eating a nutritious meal, talking with your teacher, or the wagging welcome from your dog.

2. Express yourself and cultivate gratitude by thanking others for what they do that brings happiness. Don't just do it mentally—they cannot read your mind! Practice sincerely saying thank you to at least one person each day ... "Great initiative, Pam" to a work colleague ... "Mom, that was delicious. Thanks for baking the cookies" daughter to mother ... "Dad, I am so happy you were able to come for my school play" son to father ... "I liked how you helped by collecting your friend's homework from school and dropping it off at his home" mother to son.

3. Be in the moment and feel how fortunate you are in so many ways. Count your blessings.

4. Look at what you have and not at what you don't have.

5. Write an appreciative note of thanks, via post, email, or text.

Notice the emotions of happiness move through your body when you are appreciating and showing your gratitude. It is a tingling feeling of joy. Your compliment and appreciation will be accepted well if the person you are giving them to is comfortable and loves himself. That is an art in itself, the giving and receiving of compliments and the joyful feeling that arises from both.

Cultivate the seed of gratitude into a blossoming plant. Gratitude brings out the best in us, and the good that takes place in our life, in turn, brings peace, love, and happiness.

We all look for peace in our lives, but what is peace? To some peace is accepting yourself the way you are and opening to the perfections and imperfections that are part of you. For me, peace means to surrender, to awaken to the truth of all that I am. Letting go of the fear, of the struggle, and of creating imaginary blocks. It doesn't mean giving up, but instead, opening to the bounty within me with a sense of joy.

Fill up with love for yourself and others, be mindful of the beauty within and externally, accept the happenings. Continue to flow, feel calm, and experience the peaceful sensations descend upon you.

When one lets go of anger; overcomes fear and doubt; releases the emotions of hate, vengeance, and guilt and replaces them with the positive emotions of love, peace, joy, and gratitude; then one is in a healthier and happier state. This change may not happen overnight, but the desire to make that replacement results in your transformation and greater happiness.

How did I let go of anger and overcome my fears? I went out and bought myself a single, bright-colored, helium balloon and wrote on it with a marker. I wrote in capital letters, the negative emotions I wanted to release. I went out into an open space and let the balloon go. It went higher and higher into the sky, so high that it disappeared from sight. With this act, I told myself that I was letting go of the painful emotions that were holding me back and causing unhappiness. Releasing the balloon symbolized my freedom from the negative emotions, and reaffirmed my love and faith in myself. It was a chance to start afresh and fill myself with the beauty around me.

Leap forward, and trust that you will thrive with an increase in joy and abundance. Fill yourself with the beauty of you and of what surrounds you. Be open to being on a higher frequency or becoming a higher version of yourself, and to becoming empowered. We all are given a chance to be curious, learn, thrive, and seek our potential. It is your life to mold and create. In the chapters that come, you will learn many techniques to help you achieve the transformation we have been talking about. The first step is to want it and commit to it.

Questions for Your Journal

1. Write about your present situation in your journal. What are your frustrations, anxieties, and stresses?

2. What can you do for each one of the above to let go and find peace?

3. Picture yourself letting go of the negative things holding you back. Shift your view to loving yourself. Say out aloud: "I am letting go of what is troubling me and moving toward a life of peace." After you try this technique, write in your journal about what you experienced.

Chapter 4

A Recipe for Pure Happiness

Whether you take up a hobby with a passion, exercise to keep yourself mentally and physically healthy, fuel your body with the right nutritional food, surround yourself with supporting and loving friends, or revel in the beauty of nature, these are the simple pleasures of life. And these things make for pure happiness. Let me share this recipe for happiness in detail.

HOBBIES

All of us have daily challenges, whether at school, work, rearing children, or caring for our parents, and we tend to get caught up ·in the rat race. We do not stop to think about what will help us connect our mind and body to have the outcome of happiness.

I often hear from my friends that the boss was so pushy today, or their employees don't listen to them. The tiring commute, the competition of meeting goals and demands, start to take their toll. It would be wonderful to have a hobby and make time for yourself. It would reduce your stress. There's such a wide variety to choose from—something to please every unique taste.

Sometimes parents get so caught up in caring for their children that they make no time for themselves. Being able to take time for you and pursuing an interest or hobby will bring satisfaction and a feeling of enjoyment. This, in turn, makes for a better, happier, more relaxed parent.

Here are some benefits of having a hobby:

- It encourages us to focus on a non-work task. The mind can focus on something that makes us happy and engages us.

- It gives us a sense of purpose and provides an opportunity to learn and explore something of interest.

- Completing a hobby project gives you a sense of satisfaction. A hobby can keep you interested, enthusiastic, and feeling good for years on end.

- A hobby develops self-confidence as we master a particular field, and gives us more understanding of who we are.

A RECIPE FOR PURE HAPPINESS

A hobby can be something you do by yourself, or something you do as part of a group or team. It is an opportunity for like-minded people to come together. Nowadays, with all the information on the net, we can learn anything we put our heart into.

Personally, I enjoy drawing, painting, and reading. What are your special interests? What are you passionate about? What would you enjoy doing? Think about what makes you feel happy, what interests you, and what you want to learn more about and might like taking part in.

A hobby can get you excited to learn. There are a variety of hobbies that you can avail yourself of by searching the internet or talking with friends and family. Below is a list of hobbies to inspire you with possibilities*. Try to choose something that will hold your interest and that is appropriate for you in terms of place, age, time, personal gratification, and commitments. If you try out a hobby and find you don't like it, try another one!

* Source:http://www.notsoboringlife.com/list-of-hobbies/

Arts and Crafts
Airbrushing, beadwork, bonsai, calligraphy, ceramics, embroidery, needlepoint, origami, painting, photography, pottery, scrapbooking, sewing, sketching, woodworking

Board Games
Backgammon, card games, chess, mahjong

Collecting
Antiques, art, coins, rocks, sports cards, stamps

Indoor Activities
Aquariums, cooking

Models
Cars, planes, railroads, rockets, ships

Musical
Beatboxing, choir, composing, dancing, playing an instrument, singing

Outdoor Activities
Bird watching, butterfly watching, boating, camping, fishing, frisbee, gardening, hang gliding, hiking, mountain climbing, remote-control cars and boats, walking

Sports
Archery, baseball, bicycling, bowling, football, golf, swimming, tennis

Volunteering
Building houses, food pantries, reading to the elderly, working at charities

Human nature is such that we tend to compare even our hobbies with each other, and our egos play out wondering whether we are the best, or if someone is better than we are, or how can we get to be as good as someone else. Remember that the hobby is for you, for your pleasure. You are unique, and everyone has a special gift. There is no need to compare yourself with others. Learn more from those who are expert, and interact positively with them, but don't try to be like them or be better than them. Continue with what interests you, and don't worry about what people have to say. Let go of jealousy and envy, and pursue your own path of interest and finding joy.

If you are a parent, think about encouraging your children to find hobbies. Kids today have little time to play or rest. They are so focused on tests and homework, and sometimes even are stressed from lack of sleep. The competition to build their resume, to look stellar, overwhelms students. Kids spend their free time surfing the web, or on social media, with little face-to-face communication. Parents need to guide children to take good care of themselves, to make time for healthy and wholesome recreation, and to value themselves and others. Taking up a hobby is a great way for kids to do all of those things. Show them how to make time for themselves and take up something they are passionate about—a hobby that they can carry into adulthood.

Questions for Your Journal

1. What hobby do you have?

2. List a few hobbies that interest you.

3. How do you plan to make time for a hobby?

FRIENDS

What would we do without our buddies and friends? We all should be our own best friend, but we all need some social interaction, too. We need people to create our memories with, to laugh and cry with, to be ourselves with ... people who share our secrets and our feelings.

In many societies, men are taught to mask their emotions. If they cry or discuss their problems, they are looked down upon and do not fit the standard of what is expected of a man. I was so touched and happy when Roger Federer, the all-time tennis champion, won his twentieth grand slam in the Australian Open 2018. He showed the world it is okay to shed a few tears. His father, his biggest fan, welled up with tears, too. It is a different era, where it is acceptable to cry and release your emotions of sadness and happiness. Whatever you feel within you is the true you, so be authentic and honest with yourself. This will result not only in a better relationship with yourself, but more authentic relationships with your friends and family.

Find the bright stars who bring out the best in you and are attuned to your wavelength of thought and being. Have them in your life to celebrate your joys and hold your hand in the days of sorrow. With them, you know that you are not alone, and you feel reassured and supported.

I am fortunate and filled with gratitude for friends who understand me and share and create memories with me through the happy and challenging times. They are the beautiful rays of sunshine in my life. I am fortunate and grateful to have both my son and daughter as my close friends, too.

I was bedridden, looking out my window at the blue sky and beautiful nature outside. I lay there wondering when the sun would set and I could close my eyes. I felt a sense of happiness and hope when my close friends visited and sat by me. They told me uplifting stories and took care of buying my groceries and driving my children to their after-school activities. Most of all, they were there to hold my hand through those difficult times. I am and will always be grateful for this bright circle of friends. I am so fortunate to have them in my life. Now I can enjoy the short times spent together, and we laugh, smile, and occasionally draw and paint together. In the dire times, the love of my family and friends, and my love for them, motivated me to find my way out of the bedridden state.

Research has shown that good friendships promote happiness. Friends are an integral part of our lives. They come and go, but we especially look for friendships that are long and meaningful.

Having a genuine friend and being a friend is a two-way street. One has to work at it. A friend is one who listens to you, doesn't hurt or put you down, but lifts you up, someone who walks with you in times of joy and sorrow. They are not judgmental of you, but occasionally they have to take a firm stand to help put you back on the right path.

Each one of us wants to have at least one friend who understands us and relates to us in good and bad times. Cherish yourself and your friends. Go out there and have fun with them, and let them know how much they mean to you. And remember to keep loving yourself for who you are, for you are unique.

Questions for Your Journal

1. Do you have a good friend? List the names of the friends you are grateful for.

2. What are the qualities you cherish in your friends? Next to each name, write down what makes that person wonderful.

NATURE

Nature is a healer. Spending time in natural surroundings soothes your mind and body. Research shows it reduces stress and helps improve the immune system. For endless hours we sit in front of our computer monitors and television screens. It's a good idea to go for a walk, observe the plants, trees, streams, ocean, and take in nature around you. It improves your mood and helps you unwind and relax.

On weekends, many of my friends enjoy hiking, going to parks, and puttering in their gardens. They come back feeling happier and more content. Winter is dark and gloomy with the cold, snow, and short days, so it's harder to take nature walks regularly. If the weather is bad outside, I take a blanket and sit near an indoor plant and read, or play board games with the family, laughing and enjoying each other's company.

As spring awakens, the sun shines, the flowers blossom, the birds sing, and your heart leaps with a happier thought and mood. During spring and summer, go outside with a blanket to sit on, a book to read, or music to listen to, or go out with your family or friends for a picnic lunch, playing games and enjoying the day in nature under the sun. If there is a beach nearby, pack the essentials and head out toward the sun, sand, and ocean waves. I walk daily with my dog in a place with beautiful trees and flowers and come back with a sense of peace and joy, having been in all that beauty.

If you can't go out, be creative and set up a picnic in your backyard or your apartment balcony with a few plants, blanket, music, and food, or just go out there to relax and unwind. Have some potted plants at home which bring in the feeling of nature, especially during the winter months

Questions for Your Journal

1. How does nature make you feel?

2. Go for a walk and observe nature. Write down how that affected your mood

TRAVEL

Try to take a break from the everyday routine by going for a walk or planning small day trips or, if possible, some fun travels. Detaching yourself from the daily environment gives you a fresh perspective. It makes you appreciate and understand what you have, and you return with more eagerness and enthusiasm.

When I was young, my mother used to plan our vacations to nearby places, away from the concrete jungle. Every few months we took a trip to the hill station where it was a bit cooler than in the muggy, polluted city. We enjoyed the feeling of running around, seeing new places, eating out, and just being family. Being away and together as a family is a chance to unwind, relax, and then return with a feeling of ease and joy. It helps you reset, both mentally and physically.

Travel if you can … a day trip, a camping trip, a trip across the country, or international travel. Traveling changes your perspective, bringing you back with fresh thoughts and rested mind as you return to your daily routine. It brings joy and reduces stress. Traveling

75

stimulates learning, open-mindedness, and appreciation of other cultures.

As a girl, with my parents, I flew halfway across the world from a safe and comfortable suburb. I was venturing into an unknown culture: the Big Apple, with its tall buildings, pulsating excitement, and famous celebrities ... a melting pot of different cultures and one of the most populous cities in the world. I could feel my heart beat with anxiety, but I let go of fear and started to enjoy traveling. It became a dream of mine to be able to see and experience new wonders and people of different cultures.

When my first child graduated from four competitive years at a well-known university, I suggested a gap year. During that time, he could take up a paid internship and also travel internationally by himself. It would be a chance to broaden his horizons, make new friends, learn about other cultures, and also learn to budget by living at youth hostels. I wanted him to see the world with his own eyes, grow in confidence, and learn to face obstacles and the excitement, too, that comes with travel. He was a young teenager, and with his large backpack strapped on his shoulders, he hugged us and waved goodbye, bound for new adventures. This experience was life-changing for him and for us. We let him go, even though as parents we were slightly apprehensive. He grew by leaps and bounds and came back more mature and worldlier. Now he and his wife love traveling, and they come back happier, with so many new experiences and adventures.

Many of us keep ourselves within the safe zone or the place we live in, not venturing into the unknown or onto a different path. The first time you travel, you are eager to go out again, and you become more confident. Your fears and doubts tend to disappear, and you can handle situations readily with a feeling of assurance and certainty.

International travel can help you learn so much. It immerses you in a different culture by way of food, traditions, clothes, and entertainment. It can help you better understand differences in people but at the same time the similarities of all people in the world.

Accepting other cultures and uniting the world is more intensely learned with travel than by reading.

I wanted my children to travel in order to better understand and accept themselves. My daughter traveled to Costa Rica and came back with adventurous stories to tell. To travel is to step outside of your boundaries, to interact with all kinds of people, to explore different values and cultures, and to develop more clarity of who you are. You get to know your capabilities, and you let go of your fears. You also learn different ways of looking at things, prompting you to reconsider some of your former assumptions.

I wish each one of you get the chance to explore and travel and build a strong backbone of confidence and joy, learning more about yourself than you ever imagined you could. Happy travels!

Questions for Your Journal

1. Describe the most interesting place you have traveled to.

2. What do you like and not like about traveling?

3. How could you make traveling more enjoyable?

PETS

For some people, pets like a dog or a cat can reduce stress. When they are tiny and young, pets are a big responsibility, but once they are well-trained, animals are such a joy. We make excuses that we do not have enough time to exercise or go for a pleasurable walk. Our pets convince us otherwise. For me, it is my dog who encourages me to walk daily and to play with him. I feel my stress level go down just holding him in my arms or having him beside me. He follows me and keeps glancing at me with such adoration and absolutely no judgment. He waits by the door, sparkly-eyed, with his tail wagging at the speed of light, eager to greet me. Research shows that being with a close-bonded pet reduces stress and leads to happiness and a stronger immune system.

Many hospitals and retirement facilities now allow dogs and cats to visit the patients and seniors. The people feel happier and calmer, by getting to pet and talk to a loving animal. Pets reduce the feeling of loneliness and sadness. I took my darling dog to visit my senior dad at the rehabilitation home. With such joy, the little animal licked his face and hands, and my dad's face lit up.

Pets can genuinely be a loving bond of joy and peace. There are advantages in owning a pet, but before you get one, do consider your circumstances: where you live, the time factor, and if it is right for you now. Know that an animal requires daily love and care, for all the years of its life. It is a long-term commitment and not a decision to be made on a whim. It breaks a pet's heart when its owner abandons it or sends it off to a different home. Regard your pet as part of your family, and make up your mind to keep it for its entire lifespan. A good pet owner would not discard a pet any more than she would discard one of her children.

Questions for Your Journal

1. Would you consider getting a pet? Why or why not?

2. If you would consider it, what would be the right animal for you?

GIVING BACK

Feel the joy of giving back to your friends, your community, or the world. Research shows that our brain's pleasure system is activated when we help someone else. Our feelings of joy are enhanced in giving back. We feel a sense of purpose and happiness.

Giving back can be done in different ways. It could be in the form of time, money, food donations, service, or any altruistic act that is beneficial to the giver and to the one who receives.

It is known that the happier one is, the more altruistic one is. There are many ways in which you can give back. When you give, you are in a state of feeling good. The gratitude you feel within, and the gratitude you encounter, makes you even happier.

In my situation, where I cannot go to the organizations to give my time, I feel happy assisting people and especially children by speaking with them over the phone, trying to understand their situations, and guiding them to a better life. One learns to give without expecting, and this itself brings a rush of happiness.

There are lots of ways that you can give back. Here are a few suggestions:

- Find a charitable organization you admire, and donate your money, time, or service.

- Set up a fundraiser at work.

- Involve your community members in something inspiring, like clearing the beach of litter.

- Bring food to an elderly person or someone who is lonely or homebound.

- Brainstorm with neighbors how to set up safe neighborhoods.

- Donate money to relief efforts like the Red Cross.

- Work with the local animal shelter to foster pets.

- Be part of controlled studies as a healthy individual to help medical communities.

Some of us are "naturally wired" to give back, while others have to learn seeing others in a better place brings happiness. Talk with people around you and learn what they are doing to give back. They can put you on track with a particular organization or person who needs your help. Go out there and give back!

Questions for Your Journal

1. How would you like to give back?

2. Write down how you plan to follow through.

Chapter 5

Utensils for Cooking Up Happiness

Cooking up happiness doesn't happen by accident. It requires certain utensils. Exercise, proper nutrition, laughter, and a good night's sleep are staples for any happiness kitchen. Add to that tools like journaling, a grateful diary, affirmations, visualization, and the Law of Attraction, and you'll have everything you need.

EXERCISE

Prescription: Chase the icecream truck daily. Good exercise!

As children, we were carefree—running, jumping, and playing. We did not carry out any regimented exercise. But most of us, as adults, find our lives have become sedentary. This has a negative impact on our health. To compensate for schedules that involve a lot of sitting, a formal exercise regimen inserted into the weekly routine is a good idea. This promotes happiness in multiple ways:

- Exercise generates endorphins in the body. Endorphins are called the "feel-good hormones." They kick in about half an hour after exercising and help to elevate our mood all day.

- Because during exercise the brain is fed more oxygen, exercise sharpens the mind and enhances the memory.

- Mental health is improved, and exercise can help ward off anxiety and depression. Exercise improves the immune system, making us less susceptible to illness.

- Exercise decreases stress.

- Exercise improves posture. Better posture makes you look good and feel good, which in turn increases your confidence.

- Exercise can bring on a more refreshing night's sleep. Read on, and you will find out why this is necessary for your mind and body.

- Quality of life improves, and lifespan may increase.

Society and the media place way too much emphasis on having the "perfect" body. Succumbing to media standards of beauty is foolish. We are all "the cake," however our body may be shaped, and we should love ourselves the way we are. At the same time, taking care of our bodies and maintaining a healthy weight is important for maximum happiness. Exercise helps with that.

Choosing the right workout—one tailored to your tastes and abilities—is important. If you have a workout you like, your enjoyment motivates you to do it, so think about the different kinds of exercise and choose something you think you will enjoy. Some of the many options include walking, swimming, use of a treadmill and other gym equipment, running, tennis, aerobics, yoga, power yoga, and pilates. If you have physical issues or limitations, seek the advice of a doctor, physical therapist, or personal trainer before you get started.

Beware of over-exerting! There is no need to exceed your limits, and doing so can hurt you. Listen to that sensible voice inside that tells you when enough is enough, and don't overdo it. Start exercising gradually and increase what you do over time.

I know so many young people who push their body to the limit, thinking that it is "cool." One young man lifted weights exceeding what was healthy in his first week of exercise, and pushed himself to do more than two hundred pushups in one session. The next week he was frustrated and in agony. His body could not take the abuse, but he felt he was weak and "not a man" because he didn't do better. After he calmed down, I gently held his hand and said, "It's fantastic that you've started going to the gym, but don't you think that you treated your body harshly? You may want to adjust the number of pounds you lift and the exercises you do. You can still achieve your goal of being fit and having big biceps if you learn the technique of doing it gradually, and most of all, listening to your body." He was not too happy about what I said, but I think he realized that what I told him was true. He is now fit and happy, but he understands the need to love himself, to listen to his body, and be compassionate with what it's going through at any given time.

Some of us like to exercise alone, some quietly, others with music. My husband likes to watch a television episode while exercising on his elliptical bike. Some of us monitor our time for our workout with an alarm. I have noticed many runners or walkers wearing or carrying weights while listening to music via their headphones. You can find many ways to entertain yourself and make exercising a fun and rewarding activity. Make a habit of caring for yourself and exercising to keep your mind and body attuned to a state of happiness!

Questions for Your Journal

1. How do you like to exercise?

2. Is it more fun to exercise alone or with other people?

3. Why is physical activity beneficial for you?

NUTRITION

Food powers your life, and nourishment for every cell of your body is essential. What you put into your body helps constitute who you are both physically and emotionally. Eating the right foods is consuming the fuel that keeps your body, its chemicals, brain, and other organs functioning at an optimal level.

We all feel the urge to reach out in the grocery store or when at a restaurant to eat foods that are fried or high in sugars. These block our physical and emotional energy from flowing naturally. At such moments, remind yourself that your body is precious and that nourishing it in the right way will lead you to better health and a more optimistic outlook.

Rory loved eating junk fried foods, and her daily meal was a blackened beef burger, greasy fries, and a sugary soda. To top it off, over the weekend she drank a few beers and indulged in sweet apple pie. Rory started struggling with fatigue, low energy, dull headaches, unhappy moods, and joint pain. She wondered what was happening and finally dragged herself off the couch to visit the doctor. He prescribed a range of blood tests and made a mental note of her weight gain. Once the test results came in, they showed that Rory had problems with her sugar levels, and she was in the lower range for a few essential nutrients.

She was asked to meet with a nutritionist, who taught Rory the healthy ways of eating. She was asked to eliminate sugar, dairy, alcohol, sweet beverages, and grains from her diet for a whole month. It was a struggle for Rory, but she was determined to feel better and live with more energy. She continued with this diet and learned to eat fresh vegetables, give up processed foods, cook with olive oil (known to reduce inflammation), eat organic meats and a variety of protein, drink more water, and give up sodas. Over time, the nutritionist added a few carbohydrates, like fresh fruit, to Rory's diet. Rory had learned to eat healthier, and her cholesterol and sugar levels came into balance. She could feel her energy and alertness increase, and her joint pain slowly disappeared. She learned that the right fuel for her body was essential for her happiness and well-being.

Food supports our ability to live. It enables us to move, think, and breathe. We need to take it seriously. It can benefit and sustain the body, or turn the body into a prison of suffering. There are so many diets out there, and different ideas about which one is best for us. Research the different theories, and use your best judgment. If one approach to diet does not work for you, try another, until you find the one that feels right and comfortable.

When you take a bite, consider whether the food is fuel for your "energy fire" and whether it is beneficial for your mental and physical health. Limit your use of processed foods, sugars, fast food, fried foods, and foods high in saturated fats, as these may be harmful to your body. Fresh vegetables, fresh fruits, organic meat, whole healthy grains, nuts, and polyunsaturated fats may assist you in reaching optimal health. Each of us over time knows what is right for us and what makes us feel good. Sometimes we need the assistance and guidance of a nutritionist or dietician to put us on the right path. Think of food as what powers your life. Choose wisely.

Questions for Your Journal

1. *What was your main meal today? Restaurant meal, pre-cooked, microwaved, or freshly prepared?*

2. *Would you like to improve your eating habits? Write down what foods you would like to incorporate in your diet.*

LAUGHTER AND HUMOR

How many psychologists does it take to change a lightbulb?
Only one. But the lightbulb has to WANT to change.

Laughter is a "cake's" most precious ingredient. Ripples of laughter waft in the aroma of a happy cake. Laughter and humor are known to have comprehensive benefits for both body and mind, while also enhancing our emotional health.

Children are spontaneous and can have a good belly laugh without worrying about any consequences or whether they are being watched. They laugh at the silliest things, rolling around, dancing, running, and genuinely enjoying whatever is happening. Adults around them smile and laugh along. Children are uninhibited when it comes to laughter, and they teach us to live in the moment, surrounded by magic. The sparkling effervescence of a child's uninhibited laughter is as irrepressible as soda fizz.

Laughter can help us get out of a negative mindset, and for that moment we experience the joy and vibrancy of living. When I am stressed or anxious, one of my favorite ways of dispelling that negative state is to watch a sitcom on television, laughing along loudly and fearlessly. Afterwards I am in a much happier and more positive mood. Just before I turn in for the night, I like to be in a content frame of mind and forget my worries and troubles of the day. Having a good laugh before bedtime helps with that!

Laughter relaxes our bodies and reduces the tightness of our muscles while lowering our stress hormones. Your immune system gets a boost. Your endorphins, the happy hormones known to have analgesic properties, are released to bring more joy and freedom from pain. According to scientific research, laughter can bring about a better movement of blood flow.

When we laugh with people, it reduces tension, dispels awkward moments, and eases conflicts. It relieves stress and improves our mood and that of others around us. The social benefits of laughter are many. It helps groups to bond more easily and brings about closer relationships with friends. Sometimes it attracts others to us. Laughter balances the nervous system and blocks out feelings of sadness and anxiety. We tend to forget our difficulties for that moment. Most of all, laughter expresses the essence of you, the joy that is you, into the world.

My fun times with my family are when we are all laughing and enjoying the moment together. The pleasure of being together and sharing our cheesy jokes, laughing together at our dogs and their antics, chuckling at a TV show or movie we're watching together— all this laughter forms a great bond and happy memories, too. We forget our troubles and live in the precious moment.

Any load you are carrying feels lighter when you smile. A smile is also contagious and helps bring a stronger connection between people, as a smile makes us look approachable and pleasing. Make smiling one of your habits, and in time it will become your natural state.

Be around people who make you laugh and see the beauty of life. Such people make you feel more positive and hopeful. Bask in their joy and their humor. Let yourself laugh, and make others laugh!

Try not to take yourself too seriously. Don't dwell on negative events, but move on to a better and happier state. At times we all feel the world is closing in on us. Many of us keep talking about our problems, which only brings us to a more anxious, uncomfortable state. Lighten the mood with a smile. Know that you will be able to handle the situation dealt you, but for now, be in the moment of joy and humor. Stress takes a toll on the body. Let laughter be your antidote.

Be childish, spontaneous, and magical, even if it means being in a ridiculous state of jest. Laugh straight from the heart. Double up with laughter, and you will feel the benefits.

There are many ways to find things to tickle your funny bone. You could go to a comedy club with friends, laugh at the comics in the paper, watch funny shows on television, observe laughing children, or hang out with people who make you smile. You might even join in the fun of a "laughing yoga" class!

Questions for Your Journal

1. What sort of things make you laugh?

2. How frequently do you laugh most days?

3. Do you laugh out loud or do you chuckle quietly?

4. What can you do to make yourself laugh more?

A GOOD NIGHT'S SLEEP

Shakespeare wrote this charming metaphor describing sleep: "Sweet sleep, gentle sleep, sleep that knits up the raveled sleeve of care ..."

But you don't have to be a poet to know the value of sleep. Everyone loves the feeling of falling into a peaceful slumber at the end of a long day. Restful sleep at night carries us through the new day in a better mood. Sleep is essential for a balanced emotional state. It improves the immune system, reduces stress hormones, removes body toxins, and helps us handle all situations in a better frame of mind. Sleep increases our powers of concentration and memory. It most certainly is linked to our happiness.

Here are some tips to help you maximize the benefits of sleep:

- Keep to a schedule. Go to bed and wake up at the same time each day.

- Relax before bed with a soothing routine, such as reading, taking a warm bath, meditating, or listening to soft music.

- Avoid caffeine and other stimulants before bedtime.

- Avoid having a TV, computer monitor, tablets, alarm clocks with flashing lights, or a phone, in your bedroom. Dim the lights and reduce the sounds.

- Sleep in a dark room. This stimulates production of the hormone melatonin, which helps lower blood pressure and glucose levels.

- If you are tossing and turning, get up and read or do something comfortable, and you will start to wind down.

Sleep disturbances and not having a restful, good night's sleep, can play havoc with your physical and emotional state. It is essential to have *quality* sleep to feel good about yourself.

Questions for Your Journal

1. *Are you rested or sleep-deprived? How would you feel if you could get more sleep?*

2. *What can you do to get a better and longer night's sleep?*

JOURNALING AND GRATITUDE DIARY

Writing down your thoughts is much more powerful than simply sitting and thinking, and it focuses the mind. So after you finish reading this book, keep on journaling. Write from your heart, and genuinely express your feelings.

Begin writing about your experiences daily in your journal. On the same day, write three things that you are grateful for. As you continue to do this, you will observe that you are more appreciative and aware of the simple things that bring you happiness. Filling up with the emotion of gratitude brings a soothing sense and more serenity into your daily life.

The simple daily act of gratitude can lower our stress levels and ground us for a healthier and happier life. Just as journaling is a way to get in touch with our inmost thoughts and feelings and has value for that reason, a gratitude diary helps us remember and keep track of the good things we experience. We all go through challenging hardships, but even in the midst of these we can find something to be thankful for. This kind of writing can also give you perspective as to what you want out of life.

Even if the grateful thought is small but still meaningful, such as "My friend called and told me a funny story," it brings about a sense of happiness. In time, you notice that when your brain hears more positive thoughts, that overrides the negative ones.

Studies have shown that writing down daily what we are grateful for enhances our ability to cope with difficult situations and also promotes a higher level of life satisfaction.

Here are a few suggestions of things you might write about to get your journaling and gratitude diary started:

- List three things that you are grateful for today.
- What abilities do you have that you feel thankful for? (Great listener? Dancer?)
- Even through a challenging time, what stands out that you can be grateful for?

Have fun with the journaling and with your gratitude diary! As you cultivate the habit of writing every day about what's important to you and what you're grateful for, notice how your awareness grows of your own happiness.

Questions for Your Journal

1. *Are you writing honestly or are you writing what you think others would like to read?*

2. *Do you enjoy expressing your thoughts and emotions in writing? Does this help you release the negative and assimilate the positive?*

3. *How has the journaling you've done while reading this book made a difference in your life? Do you journal with the purpose of reflecting on the challenges you face?*

AFFIRMATIONS

Affirmations are a way of turning what you desire into reality. Muhammed Ali was a big proponent of affirmations. "It's the repetition of affirmations that leads to belief," he said. "Moreover, once that belief becomes a deep conviction, things begin to happen."

And he was right. When we repeat words that affirm a positive outcome, our subconscious mind hears what we are saying. It then goes to work bringing about conditions and events that promote that outcome.

You can write your own affirmations or use those written by others. It's best to repeat an affirmation in the exact same wording, several times a day. As you drift off to sleep, upon awaking, and after meditation are particularly effective times for affirming, since the subconscious mind is most alert and responsive at those times. On those quiet occasions, mentally and softly think the affirmation. Do not say it out loud.

When you do affirmations at more active times of the day (such as in your shower or during your commute), say the affirmation out loud and with feeling. Verbalizing the words makes you *hear* what you are saying, and they start to get programmed into your subconscious. Say the words three times out loud or write them down several times. Either form of repetition is useful. Make sure your attention is on what you are writing or saying. The words are empty and useless unless your attention is there. Never fake emotion, but know that when you put genuine passion into saying the words, that makes the affirmation even more powerful.

To be most effective, an affirmation should be short and simply worded. It should state what you desire in the present tense, as if it were already a reality. For instance, a correctly constructed affirmation for better health would say something like, "I am radiantly healthy." It would not say, "I am going to be healthy very soon." If you write an affirmation in the future tense, you are telling your subconscious to keep the thing desired always in the future. Then it is always something that is going to happen someday, but of course "someday," like "tomorrow," never comes.

People sometimes ask me how I manage to live with my illness and still go on smiling with all that happens to me. I thought about this. I realized that I repeat a new affirmation until I feel it is part of me as my new truth. And I choose to do everything in the way of leading a good life in the adverse circumstances so that I can be a good role model for my children. I want to model choosing the happy path even when one has to face obstacles. We can release negative emotions, bring in the positive, and move to the next moment. Dream big, express your dreams in affirmations, and persevere toward your goals, knowing that something good awaits you.

Both my children are now wonderful young adults who have gained insight with their own experiences. They have learned to enjoy the moment in their relationships, occupations, and friendships. At the end of the day, they are grateful for what they have been given. They have chosen happiness as one of their affirmations, and I couldn't be more pleased as a mother.

Listen to your voice as you make your affirmations, and let them resonate deep within you. You will create a better life for yourself. Affirmations work best when we are focused on what we are saying and put emotion into the affirmation.

Start out affirming desires that you believe are realistic and achievable. As you attain those goals, your confidence in the affirmation process will increase. Then you will be emboldened to affirm even bigger and greater things. Don't start out by affirming things you really don't feel you can realistically ever have, be, or achieve. Instead, wait until you have more faith in the power of affirming, based on your own experiences with the process. In time you will start to believe that you can have things you always desired but never saw as possible before, and that is the time to start affirming those things.

Using affirmations can become a powerful habit. Just as negative self-talk builds negative neural pathways in the brain, repetition of constructive affirmations builds positive neural pathways. If for some reason you are unable to voice your affirmations out loud, repeat them quietly in your mind. Don't begin with too many at a time. Start out with two or three, and add one or two new ones when you begin to see some results from the ones you are already doing. Be patient, and let the process take its course and work out over time.

There is no end to the affirmations you can use or create. They are limited only by the boundaries of your imagination. Below I've suggested a few, just as samples. If they are not to your liking, I am sure you can come up with some that pertain to your own desires and circumstances.

I am attracting the perfect home for me and my family.

I feel good about me.

I am confident and believe in myself.

I am full of positive thoughts about owning a new car.

I am enthusiastic.

I work well with my colleagues.

I attract loving people into my life.

I love and accept myself for whom I am.

I understand my needs and take time to care for myself.

I love myself. I am my own best friend.

I love my body, mind, soul, and spirit. I observe, listen, and am grateful.

I am the cake!

Questions for Your Journal

1. *Make up three affirmations and write them into your journal using a pencil, or write them on a piece of scrap paper.*

2. *Now look at them and perfect the wording until each is a simple statement of exactly what you want to be, do, have, or experience. Prune out any excess words. The most effective affirmations are short and to the point.*

3. *Check and make sure the affirmations contain only positives (what you want, not what you don't want).*

4. *Check and make sure the affirmations are in the present tense (as if what you want has already happened).*

5. *Once the affirmations are to your satisfaction, write them into your journal with a pen. Read them out loud to yourself with feeling.*

CREATIVE VISUALIZATION

What is creative visualization? It is where you repeatedly and vividly imagine something you want to have happen, in order to help that event come about in real life. Athletes use visualization to help them achieve peak performance. By picturing themselves flawlessly executing a difficult maneuver, they are more likely to execute the maneuver flawlessly when the time comes to actually do it.

Athletes aren't the only ones who make use of creative visualization. Speakers visualize in order to stay calm during speeches, and actors visualize to help with delivering their lines in the best way. Spiritual mentors teach visualization to help their students develop good habits and desirable character traits. Success gurus teach it to help their students achieve their goals more quickly and easily.

Visualization can be utilized in all these different ways, because what we vividly dream we can materialize. Our brain and our subconscious receive the message of what it is we desire and set the wheels in motion to make that wish come true. When we learn how to visualize correctly, the images we generate become a reality.

Visualize the activity, event or result desired

So how does a person practice this technique? It's quite simple. You just find a comfortable place to sit or lie down, where you won't be interrupted, and begin picturing in your mind what it is that you want. It could be an event you want to occur, a goal you want to achieve, or a personal trait, such as self-confidence or compassion, that you want to develop more fully.

Simply imagine yourself being, doing, or experiencing the thing you would like to be, do, or experience. Really get into it … give your imagination free reign. Imagine all the sights, sounds, smells, tastes, or tactile sensations you would expect to be there when your dream finally manifests as reality. Picture yourself inside the story, not outside looking in. For instance, if your wish is for a lovely ring you saw in a shop, visualize the ring on your finger, not sitting in the window of the shop. Visualize touching it, twisting it in a circle, pulling it off and putting it back on again. Picture how it glimmers in the lamplight. Rub your finger over it, and feel the gemstone's cool, hard texture, or visualize the luster of the gold. Are words involved in your receiving the ring? If so, vividly imagine them being said, and let yourself feel the wonderful emotions that go along with the experience.

Here is another example. Suppose your wish is for your children to be healthy and well-balanced. Picture them in front of you—laughing, happy, caring, and loving. Listen to the sounds of laughter, smell the scent of the soap after the kids have showered and the aroma of a home-cooked meal. Feel the joy of reaching out and hugging your children and the bonds of being together.

Suppose your goal is to be self-confident and to believe in yourself. Perhaps you would picture yourself walking with your head held high and your shoulders pulled back, with a smile on your face and a feeling of joy in your heart. You would see people turn to glance at you admiringly, noticing the happy, self-actualized person you are. Maybe you would skip a few steps, or hum a little song. Don't try to figure out in advance just how the visualization will go. Instead, let your imagination guide you, and have fun with it. Visualization is an extremely enjoyable experience, as well as a very effective one.

The more real and detailed the experience is in your imagination, the more powerful the visualization will be, and the sooner it will manifest in your life as a reality. Repeat the visualization two or three times a day until the dream comes true. As with affirmations, the best times for visualizing are after meditation, just before falling asleep, or just as you awaken.

Sometimes it takes a bit of time, but with patience and repeated visualization, things turn around and start to happen. Don't lose heart or give up. Persevere and keep picturing what you want in vivid detail. For extra oomph, try combining an affirmation with each visualization. Repeat the affirmation at the start of your session, then let your imagination take over.

Daily practice of creative visualization can help you achieve your goals and turn your dreams into reality. Take each goal and focus on it with this powerful tool and learn to enjoy the beauty of this magical resource.

Questions for Your Journal

1. *Make a list of three things you would like to manifest as realities in your life. They could be things you would like to be, do, achieve, or experience.*

2. *Go to a place where you will not be disturbed. Sit or lie down and close your eyes. Then allow yourself to imagine the first scenario you would like to have happen, as if it were playing out in real life. Make it like a movie, but make sure you are in the movie, not outside watching it. Picture the event in vivid detail, involving your senses. Afterwards, write in your journal about what you experienced.*

3. *Now do the same with the other two things on your list. When one of your visualization goals manifests in real life, write about it in your journal.*

PICTURES AND POSTERS

Akin to visualization is the practice of making pictures or posters of what you want, and focusing on those images. The images make an impression on your subconscious mind, and encourage it to turn them into reality.

Some people like to draw and color images of what they desire on a large card or piece of paper. Others prefer to find pictures in magazines or in the family photo album that depict what it is they are after. They cut these out and paste them on paper, as a sort of poster or collage. You can make one card or one poster for each of your desires, or combine several desires in one card or poster (sometimes referred to as a vision board).

Once you have created your card or poster, put it someplace where you can look at it frequently. Pinning it to a wall beside your bed or taping it to the bathroom mirror can be useful. If you live with other people and want to be more private about what it is you are working on, put cards or posters in a folder that you keep in a drawer. Take them out at bedtime and look at them again when you first wake up in the morning. Just gaze at the images quietly and let yourself feel the joy and positive emotions that gazing at the pictures generates.

I like to cut out pictures and glue them on a sheet of paper, placing them the way I want things to happen. I put this poster in a prominent place so that my subconscious is frequently reminded. If I want to change or add anything to what I would like to happen, I add more photos or writing to the existing poster. For example, when I was bedridden, I cut out a picture of me walking in a field of flowers with my husband and dog. It did happen, and in a few weeks, I visited the beautiful flower gardens with my husband and dog, and best of all I was walking again!

Questions for Your Journal

1. *Make a list of three desires you especially want to work on. Decide if you will draw colorful pictures to represent these goals, or if you will cut and paste existing images onto a paper or card.*

2. *Where will you place your cards or posters so that you will see them frequently? Write down what you plan.*

3. *After working with your cards or posters for a while, write down what you experience. How do you feel when you gaze at the images?*

4. *What changes do you notice happening in your life that you attribute to this practice, or to the other practices you've been experimenting with (affirmations, visualization, etc.)?*

Statements of Intent

Quantum physics deals with the tiniest of tiny energy particles, called quanta. Everything in the universe is made up of energy, whether it's a tree, a mountain, your body, or a star. Even thoughts are made up of energy, and through energy, everything in the universe is interrelated. Since thoughts consist of energy particles, it is possible to use thoughts to attract to ourselves other forms of energy—such as desirable situations, people, or objects.

This power of the mind to attract to itself what it thinks about is called the Law of Attraction. Whatever thought-energy you project into the universe, you will receive it back as corresponding energy in the form of situations, people, or things. If you are in a happy mood and feeling positive, seeing things favorably, you are projecting those good feelings into the world and, in turn, attracting more positive energy. But if you are complaining, angry, unhappy, and sending out negative vibrations into the universe, you will attract more of the same. *Like attracts like. Think good, and you will attract good.* Those are the simple precepts of the Law of Attraction.

Because of this, it's important to think thoughts that are beneficial to us. We create our own reality through the thoughts that we think.

With this in mind, let's talk about another tool (or utensil for cooking up happiness) that I like to call *statements of intent.* In this technique, you write down exactly what it is that you want to achieve, all the goals that matter to you. But you start by writing down what you do *not* want. Here is a sample list:

I don't want to be ill anymore.

I don't want to have high expectations of others and judge people.

I don't want to fight with my spouse over petty things.

I don't want any more obstacles in my path to starting my own business.

After compiling your list of what you *don't* want, revise it into positive statements about what you *do* want, like this:

I have radiant health.

I reduce my expectations of others, judge them less, and send them love.

I appreciate my spouse and let small issues slide.

Opportunities open to me that support the start of my own business.

In revising your list of what you don't want into a list of what you do want, you replace your negative thoughts with positive ones. That allows the universe to channel positive energy to you.

Create your intention statements with focus and clarity. Be expansive in your thought, be creative, and dream big, but stay within the bounds of reality. Don't worry what others will think of you on account of the things you desire. You have been given this abundant life as a canvas on which you are to paint the picture that *you* desire to see. Be very clear about your intentions, and send them out to the universe. In its abundance, the universe will attract them to you. Energy moves in many directions and sends out many confusing messages if you are not entirely clear about what you want, so focused, precise intentions are important.

Once you've compiled your list, allow the universe to do its job. Let go of asking and start expecting. Do not get obsessed and overwrought wondering when and how it is going to happen. That part is not up to you. Your job is to have the intention and then to perform actions that will help move you toward your goal. But it's not your job to decide just when and how your dreams will be achieved. That part is in the hands of something bigger than you.

Also pay attention to subtle messages the universe may send you. These sometimes come in surprising, odd ways … some words you see on a sign, a date that has particular significance to you, a song played that has special meaning, or a gut feeling you suddenly get. This is called synchronicity, and it often comes as an answer to a question you have, or as confirmation that the universe has heard your intention and is working to make it a reality.

I experienced this synchronous moment when I was at one of my lowest points struggling with my health. I received an email titled "Unsinkable Bounce Back System" – this led me to Sonia Ricotti and her simple but powerful teachings that laid the foundation for me to turn my life around.

Once you have clearly listed your intentions, you have to feel as though they have already been achieved in the present. Trust in the universe to fulfill its part of the bargain. Allow yourself to imagine the wonderful outcomes you desire. Visualize them and affirm them, using the techniques we talked about earlier. Feel gratitude in advance for all the good that is coming your way.

"The key to bringing something into your experience that you desire is to achieve vibrational harmony with what you desire. And the easiest way for you to achieve vibrational harmony with it is to imagine having it. Pretend that it is already in your experience. Flow your thoughts toward the enjoyment of the experience, and as you practice those thoughts and begin to consistently offer that vibration, you will then be in the place of allowing that into your experience." ~Abraham-Hicks, © by Jerry & Esther Hicks

When you find a vibrational alignment between what you want and who you are, and honestly maintain it for some time, you are on the right path. The more good thoughts you put out, the more your thoughts align with a higher vibrational frequency.

You are the magnet. Align with the universe, and the good you send out will be sent back to you. Have faith in yourself, because you are worthy, and also have trust in the universe. Know that the Law of Attraction is working for you!

I have realized the miracle of this Law of Attraction. I wrote down my own statements of intent and made minute changes along the way. I jotted down about twenty intentions. I admittedly have some limiting beliefs and patterns that still have to be changed and cleared. But out of those twenty intentions, at least five took no time at all to become a reality. I wish I had known about this a long time ago!

Flow with the universe, not against it! Life is so wondrous and giving!

With this miraculous and all-supporting universe, you can ask what you desire, because the universe is abundant, generous, and unlimited. Go on. Try it!

Questions for Your Journal

1. *What do you tend to complain about often? Write down your most common gripes.*

2. *Do you observe a pattern, habit, or belief in those complaints—whether in your relationships, family life, work, health, or finances— which you would like to change? Write down what that is.*

3. *Use your gripe list to help you create your I-don't-want list. Write it down in your journal.*

4. *Next, turn your I-don't-want list into an I-want list: a statement of positive intentions. Write it in your journal, then read it aloud to yourself with gratitude, as if it has already happened.*

5. *Some goals need nothing but spiritual tools like visualization and affirmation in order to become reality. Other goals require action on our part, action in the physical world. Look at each of your goals. Which ones require action in the physical world? Write down those that do, and next to them write down very specifically what your action(s) will be.*

6. *If you notice any synchronous moments or "messages from the universe," write these down in your journal as they occur.*

Chapter 6

From Overwhelm to Serenity

Can we make changes to our brain at any age? You ask me if you can do it now, and I say yes! When we are young children, our brains are like sponges that absorb and learn quickly and efficiently. You are not too old to make changes by rewiring your brain. With advances in neuroplasticity and neuropsychology, we are able to optimize performance and achieve our goals by working on our mental and emotional skills. This helps us create new patterns and release the old, disempowering ones.

I stood at a podium. Hundreds of people looked back at me from the audience. My heart started racing like a combustion engine. My palms were sweaty, my throat dry, and I wondered if I could utter a word. Screaming, I sat up in bed. I realized this was a dream, or should I say, a nightmare. This fear of mine was being lived in a recurring dream like a movie repeatedly playing. We all have fears, and they keep playing out in different circumstances and situations. Wouldn't you like to move toward your fear and face it head on? That's what you learn to do when you study techniques to reprogram your brain.

Our fears are built into our brain patterns and the patterns of our nervous system. To break free of these, we learn through neuroplasticity. Neuroplasticity is a favorite buzzword today and an umbrella term that refers to the brain's ability to change continuously throughout our lives. The brain can reorganize itself to form new connections between brain cells and new neurological patterns that affect our thinking, emotions, behavior, and environment.

Social norms and cultural values, taught to us since the start of our lives, have been ingrained in our brain and encoded in our subconscious. Also encoded are beliefs about ourselves developed in our childhood, many of which are self-sabotaging. In an earlier chapter, we talked about how the subconscious tends to follow the patterns it was taught during our earliest years. This is what it knows to do, being ingrained with those patterns. With neuroplasticity, we can unhinge and remove the deep-seated beliefs that are not beneficial to us and recode them with new and more advantageous patterns that support us.

NEUROPLASTICITY

Meditation, mindfulness, visualization, affirmations are all ways of increasing the plasticity of the brain and bringing about upgradeable and multifaceted change. A program founded by John Assaraf, called "Neurogym," is another way to reprogram your brain. He teaches specifically how to retrain and reprogram it. I listened to John's insightful webinars, knowing that this could be beneficial for my health and emotional well-being. I enrolled in Neurogym's "Winning the Game of Fear Retraining Program" with a bit of apprehension, but more with a feeling of underlying excitement.

The program teaches you to exercise your brain or "neuro muscles" with daily mental and emotional aerobics called "innercise." This strengthens your emotional and mental "core muscles." It develops self-confidence, improves self-esteem, and empowers you with stronger and more beneficial mental and emotional patterns. With innercise, you learn to break away from the negative beliefs of fear. With this daily habit, you begin to let go of your disempowering habits and move toward achieving your highest potential. This clears the path to what we so richly deserve: happiness, success, and a sense of freedom.

My perceptions, worries, embedded patterns, and excuses have changed with my daily innercise, as I work on rewiring my brain. I have released many of my fears, changing the way I act in certain situations and learning to better appreciate myself.

There are four different levels of the program. Each is designed for a person to follow at least ten days. I was initially apprehensive during level one, but in a couple of days looked forward to my innercises. I wrote down my fears and chose the one that resonated as the biggest one at that time. I honed in on visualizing the fear, which brought about sensations of the fear itself, but this disappeared with listening to John Assaraf's calming voice. I spoke out my affirmations and moved forward to priming my subconscious with new patterns. In a week's time, I was on to a better path of success and self-worth, by letting go of my fears.

The second level was a bit more intense for me. I took a gap day and rested and then resumed with my innercise the next morning. This path to success can be achieved, with letting the fears change into a feeling of excitement.

During the third level, I felt I was in a trance, where everything within me was calm and settled. In this level, John Assaraf asked us to let go of our unconscious fears without even being aware of what they are. You learn to let go of the unconscious fear, and then, with his soothing voice, he guides you through beneficial affirmations toward achieving success. During the third level, I felt serene and calmer within. This feeling continued, and it has made a remarkable change in my behavior toward being more productive and motivated while being able to handle my stressful situations with aplomb.

Level four is mostly dedicated to making the change of breaking the old patterns and replacing them with positive, beneficial ones.

Neurogym offers insightful bonus presentations by world-known brain experts. You also have the opportunity of joining a Facebook group, Neurogym Achievers, which is led by John Assaraf, his team, and Mark Robert Waldman, a leading neuroscientist.

Life has opened in more marvelous ways with the fears being deleted from my earlier programmed brain. I am truly a higher version of myself, forging forward, meeting the fears, and changing them into excitement and positive action. With this program, I do my daily innercises, thereby strengthening my neuro muscles, and I'm learning to change the way I behave and handle my emotions and situations as they come up in a difficult situation. I am learning to break away from those patterns that were disempowering and to create new, more beneficial ones which are now being encoded in my subconscious.

I would like to thank John Assaraf and the Neurogym team for being so kind as to let me share my experience with you. If you have a chance to follow this program, I suggest the time is now to make the change.

I was fascinated with the idea that we could reprogram our brains and went further to read and understand this great advancement called neuroplasticity. I discovered Sarah McKay, an Oxford-educated neuroscientist and a brain-health commentator, who offers a technique called "REFIRE to Rewire Your Brain." This is explained in her blog at www.yourbrainhealth.com.au and in her online course at www.theneuroacademy.com.

Dr. McKay has made advancements in neuroplasticity. Here are her REFIRE steps to follow for reprogramming the brain:

R for *Reason*
Clearly understand the REASON why you would like to change a mental or emotional pattern, belief, mindset, or behavior. Having clarity about the goal brings on excitement rather than doubt and fear. Once you know your purpose, break it down into micro-goals, which make the master goal easier to reach. Achieving the micro-goals rewards your nervous system with dopamine (a neurotransmitter that controls the brain's pleasure-and-reward centers). This motivates you along the way to attaining your goal.

E *for Engage*

ENGAGE in a behavior, skill, or task that you are keen to learn. Focus yourself on the job, and be single-minded. Support from a mentor or coach may bring out motivation from within you.

F for Feel
FEEL and find that sweet spot of your emotions in between fear (over-arousal) and boredom (under-arousal). This is the optimal state in which to learn. Learning is impaired in both the states of fear and boredom. If you are bored, then you are under-aroused and maybe need to set a bigger goal. If fear seems to be sabotaging your chances, perhaps you need a more moderate goal better suited to your present skill level. The right amount of excitement stimulates the cortisol hormone, giving you the push to be in the flow and moving toward your goal.

I for Imagine
IMAGINE and clearly visualize yourself physically carrying out the task, and feel the sense sensations associated with this picture. Imagining an activity activates the same regions in the brain as doing the activity does. Visualize how you will respond emotionally to achieving your goal. Also clear the hurdles in your way by imagining them dissolving.

R for Repeat
This is the stage where people seem to give up. If you are unable to do the task, you must circle back and go through the steps to REPEAT, and repeat to achieve. As Sarah McKay says, "Neurons that fire together, wire together. Neurons that are out of sync fail to link." As we have heard, 'Practice makes perfect," so keep repeating and practicing the new behavior or mindset.

E for Extend
EXTEND and keep repeating until you cannot get it wrong. Repeating the task is one thing, but you need to practice on the cusp of your highest potential or ability. Why are Olympians who they are? They practice until they can't get it wrong. Sheer hard work, want, and will are required for the neurons to refire and rewire.

A simple example of "extending" for you to try, is juggling two balls. If you can't do it, practice throwing one in the air and catching it until you are perfect at it. Then add the second ball and try to juggle until you can catch them both. When you have achieved this, then you have reached your micro goal, and will feel a rush of dopamine, the "reward hormone." Then go ahead and add a third ball, and try to juggle all three. Success requires wanting and perseverance. If when you add the third ball you are unable to juggle, go back and repeat the previous stages and then try again to add the third. Observe how your brain gets refired to rewire by reaching that sweet spot between under-stimulation and over-stimulation.

Here is the REFIRING image by Sarah McKay from her website:

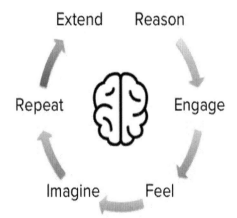

REFIRE: 6 steps to rewire your brain
(and master anything)

Extend   Reason

Repeat   Engage

Imagine   Feel

Questions for Your Journal

1. What do you want to change concerning your habits and beliefs?

2. What do you need to do to release the old habits and bring in the new ones you desire?

3. Do you think that you need someone as a mentor to help you with this? If so, who might be a good mentor for you?

4. Pick one of your goals, and apply the REFIRE technique to achieving it. Write about your experiences as you do this.

MEDITATION

"The quieter you become, the more you hear," said Ram Dass, one of the popular spiritual gurus of the 1970s. In our modern society with its pressures and busy times, we find ourselves inundated with information, making it difficult to be calm and at peace. Meditation is a way to reduce this overload and bring about awareness and inner serenity.

Originating in India, Japan, and the various South Asian countries, meditation has gained popularity worldwide. Research suggests that meditation helps with reducing anxiety and stress. It normalizes blood pressure and heart rate. It also helps us focus better and brings about more positive feelings and serenity from deep within.

Meditation is a means to train the mind so that we may discover within ourselves the deeper truths. In meditation, you listen for that profound inner silence, the space between your thoughts. The constant internal mind chatter lessens or disappears. It is an effortless process in which you let go of the object of focus or the process, as you start discovering your sincere and authentic self.

There are various methods for practicing meditation. Here is an elementary one that you may like to try.

1. Find a quiet place to sit down, and where you can be comfortable and won't be interrupted. Close your eyes gently. As a beginner, you can start meditating for just five minutes and increase the time to ten or fifteen minutes a day, twice a day.
2. Choose a word to be your "mantra." A mantra is a thought you repeat during the meditation. Choose a word that is simple and corresponds to your intention (such as *joy* or *peace*).
3. Take a few slow, deep breaths. These will help calm you and prepare you for meditation.
4. Bring your mantra to mind. Let yourself repeat it mentally. The mantra will change as you do this. It may get quieter, softer, or even become distorted. Do not try to bring it back to what it was originally. It's changing because your mind is settling to deeper levels, and this is good.
5. Thoughts will naturally come and go. The important thing is not to resist them or resent them. When you notice you've been off on thoughts, simply—and very gently—just bring your mind back to the mantra.
6. Meditation is never the same twice. Sometimes you will feel "deeper" than other times. Do not compare your meditations and judge one session as better than another. Whatever happens when you're meditating is good.
7. At the end of meditation, take a couple of minutes to slowly open your eyes and return to the world. Always come out of meditation slowly.

Now let's talk about a few other ways of practicing meditation. One of my favorite meditation teachers is Deepak Chopra, a leading spiritual teacher. Please refer to the *Recommended Resources* at the end of this book to learn more about his meditation techniques.

Another kind of meditation I really enjoy is called "Awareness of Being." In this, you take into consideration both the inner and

119

external thoughts. Internal means your memory and thoughts, while external means the senses (smell, taste, sound, etc.) The point is to experience being attentive, detaching, and being in a state of non-judgment. As the internal and external thoughts start to unfold, you observe the emotion, and in the next moment, you do the same, which may be an entirely different state or emotion. The events of our memory rise and fall, and we are to simply observe this. For example, if at the moment you are sad, you are aware of this emotion, observe, and experience it, but in the next moment you maybe sadder or maybe happier. What do you do then? You go with the flow, watch, feel, and move to the next moment. Have a neutral attitude toward whatever thoughts or feelings you experience. This cultivates a state of stillness, of being your authentic self, the awareness or consciousness that underlies all thoughts. The mind chaos subsides, the internal chatter and self-talk reduce, and you reach a state of inner peace.

"Vipassana" meditation originated in India. The word means "insight into what is happening when it is happening." Vipassana meditation was made popular by S. N. Goenka (© Vipassana Research Institute). He says, "Removing old conditionings from the mind and training the mind to be more equanimous with every experience is the first step toward enabling one to experience true happiness." He suggests that we have to be aware every moment of our feelings. To attain a mind of peace and balance, he says we need to let go of both aversion and craving, which are the root of our suffering. He teaches that we should be mindful of both our internal and external experiences, letting them arise and flow through us, and staying in the present moment.

We all want to reach the state where we feel life has shifted and changed for the better. One learns to retrain the mind, reframe the internal self-talk, release expectations, and limiting beliefs. We then experience a more prosperous and fulfilling life. As Vipassana meditation techniques are getting more popular, it is easy to avail yourself of these retreats all over the world.

I begin my day with a "Loving Kindness" meditation or "Metta" meditation." "Metta" in Pali means kindness and is part of the Buddhist tradition of compassion meditation. Here I sit quietly with my eyes closed, bringing my breathing to a stable equilibrium of equal inhalations and exhalations. Once I feel grounded and calm, I say to myself and for myself:

May I be happy
May I be loved.
May I be well
May I be at peace.
May I be safe
May I live life with ease, grace, and harmony.
I am worthy of love and choose happiness.

Following that, I send out metta or positive vibrations and thoughts by picturing the one I am sending them to. I send love to each of my children and daughter-in-law, my husband, my father, my brother, his family, and my father and mother-in-law, mentally saying, *May you be happy ... choose happiness.*

In the next step, I visualize my close friends who I am grateful to share life with, and send out positive thoughts to those individuals. Next, I send out to the community and to those I may have rubbed the wrong way or those who I feel may not be happy with me, and finally to all the world. *May they be happy ... choose happiness.*

This meditation helps me accept myself the way I am and feel empowered. It brings me peace. For people I am having a difficult time with, I send them love and happiness. I shower them with good thoughts and love, and to my own astonishment, the love comes back in forms of text messages or phone calls. They are there to help me or say something good. My vibrations genuinely do reach them. They are not my closest friends, but I feel their trust and feel happy. In this way, more peace and harmony exist in the world and get spread among people.

The other saying I chant quietly in my mind every morning is:

May auspiciousness be unto all.
May peace be unto all.
May fullness be unto all.
May prosperity be unto all.

Metta meditation helps us have a feeling of acceptance, compassion, and empathy toward ourselves and others. It also starts us on a positive footing for the day, and life's petty issues fade away. Negative mental habits, like judging or hating others, also fade away and disappear.

Another popular form of meditation today is Mindfulness Meditation, which has its origins in Buddhism. In the list of resources at the back of this book, you will find several apps that make use of Mindfulness Meditation.

Another technique, Jessi Rita Hoffman's "Master of Living" Peace Meditation, features one-on-one instruction in meditation via phone or Skype. Please refer to the *Recommended Resources* list at the back of this book.

In addition, the list has apps that provide guided meditations ... yet another form of meditating. In this sort of practice, the person listens with their eyes closed while a narrator guides their imagination from one positive thought to another.

Meditation is known to have varied emotional, physical, and mental benefits. It instills in us a feeling of serenity—emotional and psychological well-being, helping us deal with stressful situations. It reduces our inner negative thoughts and mind chatter and puts us on a path to self-awareness. Neuroscience research suggests that through regular practice of meditation and mindfulness, lower cortisol levels result, which reduces anxiety.

I was taught by an excellent yoga teacher at the beginning of any meditation to first reconnect with my breathing and to balance my inhalations and exhalations. Our breathing slows when we are relaxed and calm. It becomes shallow and rapid during stressful times.

When I find myself in situations small or significant where my anxiety levels increase, I take in a few deep breaths and release them, until I feel calmer. The science behind this is that taking a few deep breaths causes the vagus nerve to send a signal to the nervous system to lower the heart rate, blood pressure, and cortisol levels. This is a tool you can use to reduce the build-up of anxiety, and you will feel your body disengage into a more relaxed state.

Wouldn't it be beneficial if we could incorporate a meditation class into our school curriculums for our young ones and adolescents? Some schools in the world have learned the benefits of meditation. With the complex pressures put on our kids to perform their best, with the high competition, and with their need to keep up with social media, children's minds race from one thought to another. Are they really able to focus? Do they internalize the anxiety around them and tend to withdraw from society? Meditation teaches children to sit in one place, to focus better, and to be less anxious and restless. It brings on a sense of calm and happiness, and cultivates an attitude of appreciation and confidence.

With daily use of meditation over the years, I have learned to connect with myself and treat myself with loving kindness and compassion. My mind chatter and internal negative self-talk have reduced, and I feel renewed and reawakened to a more empowered and happier me.

You may like to download meditation applications on your phone or computer for easy access. Please refer to the *Recommended Resources* at the end of the book.

Questions for Your Journal

1. *Do you think that meditation would be beneficial for you? Why or why not?*

2. *Are you ready to give yourself this opportunity to learn a simple meditation?*

3. *Do you think you can make it a habit in your daily life?*

TAPPING: EMOTIONAL FREEDOM TECHNIQUE

The Emotional Freedom Technique (EFT), better known as "tapping," is a holistic tool that provides energy healing by making use of the body's meridian points. The Chinese discovered that meridians, or energy circuits, run through the body. We have many unaddressed emotional challenges which can either be on the surface or deep-rooted. These show up as a disturbance in the meridian system. With EFT, a person makes a verbal statement while tapping with their fingers on a particular meridian point to achieve the desired result.

In acupuncture, tiny needles are placed on the surface of the skin at the meridian points. EFT uses tapping fingers instead of needles to help relieve both physical symptoms and emotional issues. EFT treats the cause of problems, rather than the effect.

Research suggests that the amygdala part of the brain, which is like the alarm center of the fight-or-flight response, is quieted down with use of EFT. Tapping is like peeling back layers of the "stress onion" until no layers remain. The stress hormone, cortisol, which is produced when we are stressed or scared, is reduced with effective tapping. Harvard, Stanford, and other universities, as well as some medical establishments, are studying EFT and using this method to address their clients' and patients' issues.

According to the theory behind EFT, there are three steps or stages we go through whenever we feel a negative emotion. First we experience a distressing thought or memory, then there is a disruption in the body's energy system, and, last of all, a negative emotion occurs. Gary Craig, the original proponent of EFT, explains it this way: "If step two (the intermediate step) does not occur, then step three is impossible. In other words, if the memory does not cause a disruption in the body's energy system, then the negative emotion cannot occur. That is why some people are bothered by certain memories, and others are not. The difference is that some people have a tendency for their energy systems to become imbalanced under such memories, while others do not."

How a Negative Emotion is Caused

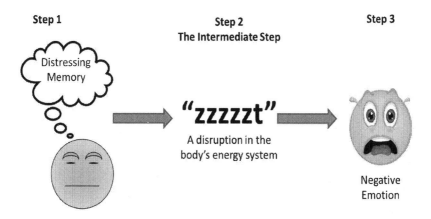

© Gary Craig (www.emofree.com)

I learned the tapping technique a few years ago but only recently started using it regularly. Now, if there is an emotional trigger that puts me off balance—like arguing with my husband, being upset about a situation, or just not working with compassion for myself— I reduce the stress by tapping. I feel calmer after having gone through a few rounds. In each round of tapping, I talk out what is bothering me. I observe how I feel afterwards and assign it a number from zero to ten, with ten indicating the most stress. If I still need to let go of the stressor, I tap another round on my end-meridian points, until I feel at ease and my thought-chaos reduces.

Sometimes I'm bothered by old, deep-rooted memories that surface and disturb me, such as memories of two miscarriages I had. In such instances, I begin by writing down what I want to address. What is it that really is troubling me, and why does it bother me again and again whenever I'm feeling low? I look deep within myself to find the root cause of these negative, recurring emotions that the memory stirs up. Then I tap into the negative feelings of guilt and pain. Regarding the miscarriages, I realized it was not my fault and I did not need to feel guilty. The body aborted the child, as maybe it was not ready to be on this Earth. I needed to forgive my thoughts and feelings associated with those experiences. In the next few rounds of tapping, I repeated how grateful and fortunate I was to have two beautiful children, my treasures of joy. During tapping, the negative emotions lifted, and I find that they rarely return. On occasion, if they do show up, I tap on them once more, removing yet another layer of that particular memory's "stress onion." Eventually, all the layers will be gone, and I will be able to remember the miscarriages without experiencing emotional pain.

I learned that we can reduce some kinds of physical pain without having to explore our emotions. But with chronic pain issues, we need to go beyond, to the emotional area associated with the pain. We must let the story unfold, while using phrases and tapping. Once we clear the issue, we are on a better position to address the reason for the pain and can replace it with more positive thoughts and affirmations.

Here is an illustration of the "tapping points"—that is, the end-meridian points where a person taps with their fingers while practicing the Emotional Freedom Technique:

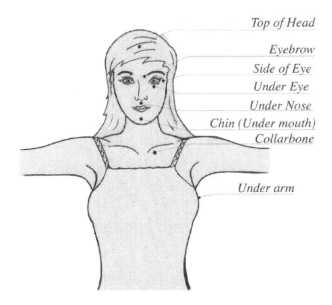

To learn the precise procedure for tapping, watch this demonstration video by Nick Ortner on YouTube:
https://www.youtube.com/watch?v=XyHxuTG6jRk

Here are the steps a person goes through when practicing the EFT technique:

1. Take a few slow, deep breaths until you are inhaling and exhaling at a steady pace.

2. Rate where you are emotionally between zero and ten, with ten being the most distressed and zero the least distressed

3. Come up with a statement or phrase that describes the negative thought that is bothering you. This statement should genuinely reflect what your subconscious believes.

4. Use the index and middle fingers of one hand (or both hands) to tap on the meridian points in the diagram above. You can tap on either side of the body or both sides, simultaneously.

Karate Chop Point

5. Start with the point that's on the side of the hand, called the "karate-chop point," and repeat your chosen phrase three times as you tap, and end it each time with "I deeply love and accept myself." For example, "Even though I am angry that I was not promoted, I deeply love and accept myself." This helps us direct compassion and love to ourselves.

6. Follow this sequence of tapping on your meridian points for one round:

> Inner part of the eyebrow
> Outer side of the eye
> Under the eye
> Under the nose
> Under the lip
> Collarbone (about one inch below the collarbone)

Under the arms (about three inches below the armpits)
Top of the head

7. Complete a few rounds of tapping. As you tap, gradually revise the phrase you started with to something more positive.

8. After each round, evaluate how you feel, giving it a score between zero and ten. Continue doing rounds until you feel the lightness and change.

Nick Ortner, Dawson Church, and Louise Hay all have created tapping sequences that you might like to use. These can be found on YouTube and in their books and audios (see *Recommended Resources* at the end of this book). I particularly recommend reading the book *The Tapping Solution for Manifesting Your Greatest Self*, by Nick Ortner. It contains a number of tapping sequences you might like to use, including this one (a favorite of mine) which he has graciously agreed to share with us:

Choosing Self-Acceptance and Self-Love

To begin, take three deep breaths.

Start by tapping on the karate-chop point. Repeat tapping on this point three times, saying, "Even though I have these old, leaky patterns, I love myself and accept myself as I am."

Eyebrow: *These patterns*
Side of Eye: *They're ingrained in me*
Under Eye: *I should be over them by now*
Under Nose: *I shouldn't still be falling into them*
Under Mouth: *But I do*
Collarbone: *I still stumble into these old, familiar, leaky patterns*
Under Arm: *I don't like that it happens*
Top of Head: *But it happens*

Eyebrow: *And that's okay*
Side of Eye: *I accept myself with these patterns*
Under Eyes: *I love myself with these patterns*
Under Nose: *It's safe to notice the emotions buried in these patterns*
Under Mouth: *I can begin to hear the limiting beliefs that fuel these patterns*
Collarbone: *And I can love myself throughout it all*
Under Arm: *There's no shame in having these patterns*

Top of Head: *They're part of my human experience*
Eyebrow: *I can look at them with a new awareness*
Side of Eye: *Without guilt or shame or self-criticism*
Under Eye: *I can see these patterns with a new eye*
Under Nose: *And I can love myself throughout the entire process*
Under Mouth: *I can accept myself throughout my entire experience*
Collarbone: *It's safe to love and accept myself now*
Under Arm: *Letting myself relax*
Top of Head: *Choosing to feel peace now*

Repeat the rounds until you feel you have achieved the desired effect.

Here is another beautiful tapping sequence (this one by Dawson Church). It helps you to be the best version of yourself as you move into your day. (Tapping World Summit © Tapping Solution and Presentation © Dawson Church EFT Universe):

I release anything and everything in my body, mind, and spirit other than the highest version of my higher power (karate-chop point twice)

I completely accept the version of me that is perceived by my higher power, and I release all other versions of me (karate-chop point)

I release anything and everything (eyebrow point)

In my body, mind, and spirit (outer eye)

Other than the version of me (under the eye)

Perceived by my higher self (under nose)

And I fill myself (chin)

131

With the version of me (collarbone)

That is perceived by my higher power (collarbone)

I am one with my higher power (under arm)

I am one with the highest possible mind (karate-chop point)

I am one with the highest possible energy in the universe (karate-chop point)

It flows through me (eyebrow)

And every single word and thought (side of eye)

That I say or think today (under eye)

My whole mind, body, and life (under nose)

Is infused with the energy and vision of my higher power (chin)

And I release everything else (collarbone)

Naturally and effortlessly (under arm)

My body and all of my potential that is held in the mind of my higher power (karate-chop point)

I fully accept that, and I move into the day knowing this is true (karate-chop point)

One word of caution: If you think that some issue is too challenging for you to handle alone and will cause emotional upheaval if you tap on it (for example: severe childhood trauma), it is better to seek help from a tapping expert than to try to remove that big emotional block on your own. To find a tapping expert practitioner, I suggest you visit these websites: https://thetappingsolution.com/eft-practitioners/ https://eftuniverse.com/certified-eft-practitioners

OTHER USEFUL METHODS

Reiki is a Japanese technique to reduce one's stress and promote healing. I have a kindhearted friend who is masterful at this hands-on healing method. During a session, she holds my feet and transfers energy to my body. I can feel the life force energy settle in me after an hour of having the session. Check out reiki!

There are many other techniques which you can research that may be beneficial to you, such as Tai Chi and Qi Gong. The ones I've shared are only a sampling of what is available. Modalities like meditating, tapping, reiki may help you find serenity in the overwhelm of life, allowing you to open up more fully to the wonders and potential within you.

Questions for Your Journal

1. What memories keep recurring for you that cause you emotional pain?

2. What recurring physical pain(s) do you have that you suspect may be rooted in emotional trauma?

Watch the YouTube video by Nick Ortner that was recommended above. Then, using your own words, try tapping about an issue that is particular to you. Write about your experience

Chapter 7

Binding All the Ingredients with Love

I have written this book in the earnest hope that you have a chance to practice and experience treating yourself with loving kindness, compassion, trust, and acceptance. Be thankful for the happenings taking place in your life. Be open to receiving them, whatever they may be. Live in the moment, with love in your heart, and you will start to attract more love. Radiate love to others. Send it out into the world to create more understanding, peace, and harmony. Fill yourself with love and let it shine, knowing we all are interlinked and enmeshed.

Unlock your powers of intention and love, and empower yourself. Go deep within and hear the whispers of your intuition. Let go of the fears, the negative beliefs, and the thoughts that hold you back. Explore the beauty and mysteries of life, the potential, and the magic that lie before you. Let go off judging yourself, and of being concerned about what others have to say.

With the realization that "I am the cake," that I am the substance itself, and that I love myself, I am no longer swayed by what society says or whether others criticize me. Life has opened up for the taking. There is a joy coursing through me that I never felt before. The world with its simple pleasures is a delight to me now ... the sun rising in the morning, the bees humming from flower to flower, my darling puppy's soft licks, the warm relationships with my close friends and family. I aspire to be in the now, to live with every waking moment with gratitude and love ... to rejoice in the wonders of life, the universe, and divine grace, which showers blessings on me. I encourage you to take up the reins of life in your hand, to fully open your eyes, and to realize the beauty within and around you. Live to the fullest and be true to yourself, treating yourself with love and patience. Be thankful for every breath you take.

I wake up in the morning using Abraham/Esther Hicks' method of attracting seventeen seconds of positivity and beauty. I start my day choosing happiness and being in the moment, as the mystery of the moment opens up to me. I sleep being grateful for the smallest of things that happened during the day. I tap, meditate, and practice my "innercises." Even in adverse times, I realize I am alive, and I am a creator who can attract and make things happen. Let's release our old patterns and replace them, bringing about more peace in our lives. Love for ourselves is the key to being empowered, to unfolding our full potential and rejoicing in life.

Love is something greater than mere romantic love. The word is used without sufficient gravitas and understanding of its meaning. We are taught that loving ourselves may be selfish or narcissistic, but without self-love, we haven't the ability to effectively love anyone else. We are all worthy of love, and we need to be open to receiving love from ourselves so that we can feel safe and comfortable with who we are.

The phrase "I love you" doesn't resonate the same for everyone. It makes some people uncomfortable. They may need to hear a different phrase, such as, "You are kind" or, "I like you." Some people are uncomfortable with a hug. As a teenager, for example, a person may have been told, "I love you" by an aunt who only voiced the words to get them to help her with her chores. If they didn't do the chores, she wouldn't say the phrase, and this upset the teenager. Now whenever she hears "I love you," it reminds her of that earlier experience.

If you find it hard to say "I love you" to yourself, find another phrase that you are comfortable with. Take your time and come up with the right phrase that will put you on the path of knowing it is all okay, and you can start telling yourself that phrase.

Many of us feel that love is something we must receive from others and must beg for. Our actions scream for attention and appreciation. Stand your ground rooted in the knowledge that you are good and loved by yourself, and don't hand over your power to someone else by basing your self-worth on whether or not they love you. I was needy of appreciation and acknowledgment, but when I learned to believe in myself, I grew comfortable with who I honestly am and now need no outside validation.

We sometimes wonder why, when we send out love to others, it is not reciprocated. This leads us to feel hurt. Try to shower the love by sending it out the way you would like to be treated. We expect our love to be returned, equally or better, and in the manner that we like and want. But realize that this does not need to happen. You may receive love back or you may not. You may receive it back in a way that is not especially to your liking. Don't let this upset your emotional balance. Be rooted in being you, brimming with love for yourself. When you are happy with you, the love will automatically spread, and you will not have any expectations of the love to be returned.

People are all at a different place in their life journey. When they are grounded and treat themselves with love and compassion, feeling secure about who they are, then maybe they can reciprocate our love. But we should not stop loving simply because someone is not emotionally mature enough to give back what we radiate. The sun radiates its life-giving warmth irrespective of how it is received. Whether or not we send gratitude back, the sun keeps right on shining. That's how we should be in our love of others. We shine no matter what. We stand strong in our love for ourselves, and radiate love to the universe. If it comes back to us from some of the people we send it to, all the better. But we do not depend on anyone for love. The sun needs no other heavenly body in order to keep shining. Let your love be like the sun, independent of anyone and anything going on around it. Then you will be happy.

Love can be sent in different ways other than saying, "I love you." You can send it out during your meditations. You can send it out in the form of a service or an action. You can send it out in the form of a food.

Love for me now is a reawakening of myself, a knowing that I am my spirit, soul, and vibrational energy, not just my physical state, and with that, I am open to receiving and becoming who I genuinely am, loving and accepting myself while radiating love to others. Love is the ingredient that binds the cake, that holds the other ingredients together. Love is the backing on the beautiful quilt called life.

Know that you are magnificent, beautiful, and loving. Love yourself, embrace life with gratitude, and spread the good, opening up the beauty of feeling free and alive. Start living now, and be the creator of your life!

The more you grow within, give back to your community. Make life more meaningful for yourself and others. Be the difference. Spread the love by volunteering or donating to a cause.

Love is the ingredient that binds the cake together. Remember what you learned in this book and stand tall and happy. Live with confidence, self-esteem, and expand your love for yourself and those around you. Go ahead: treat yourself the way you would like others to treat you, from this very moment. Use the utensils for happiness cooking and throw out the negative self-talk. Believe in the abundance and support you have from the universe and align yourself with this. Live in a state of harmony. Explore your potential, and unfold the highest version of you. Shift your mindset, and soon the outward situations will match your positive and happy inner thoughts.

Questions for Your Journal

1. What does love mean to you?

2. "Without self-love, we haven't the ability to effectively love anyone else." What do you think that statement means? Do you agree? Why or why not?

3. How has your love evolved for yourself in the process of reading this book?

4. What will you do going forward to become more loving and accepting of yourself? What will you avoid doing?

Remind yourself every day that you are deserving of all that life has to offer. Say it aloud a few times with a smile on your face and joy in your heart: "I am the cake!" Let the words resonate it in your subconscious, until it is ingrained as your belief. I believe in you, and I love you!

Recommended Resources

Now that you know that you are "the cake" and you want to continue unearthing your potential, here is a list of books, audio books, websites, foundations, retreats, lectures, and apps for you to refer to and use as valuable resources.

Journaling Worksheet: Available for download at
https://www.urthecake.com/journaling-worksheet

BOOKS

Ask and It Is Given: Learning to Manifest Your Desires, by Esther and Jerry Hicks (Hay House, 2004)

Awakening into Oneness: The Power of Blessing in the Evolution of Consciousness, by Arjuna Ardagh (Sounds True, 2007)

Boundless Energy: The Complete Mind/ Body Program for Overcoming Chronic Fatigue, (Ayurvedic principles) by Deepak Chopra (Three Rivers House, 1995)

Conscious Loving: The Journey to Co-Commitment, by Gay Hendricks and Kathyln Hendricks (Bantam Books, 1990)

Count Your Blessings: The Healing Power of Gratitude and Love, by John F. Demartini (Hay House, 2006)

Everything You Need to Know to Feel Good, by Candace Pert and Nancy Marriott (Hay House, 2006)

Forgive for Good, by Fredric Luskin (Harper, 2003)

Happier: Learn the Secrets to Daily Joy and Lasting Fulfillment, by Tal Ben Shahar
(McGraw-Hill, 2007)

I Heart Me: The Science of Self-Love, by David R. Hamilton (Hay House, 2013)

Innercise: The New Science to Unlock Your Brain's Hidden Power, by John Assaraf (Waterside Press, 2018)

Inspirations: Your Ultimate Calling, by Wayne Dyer (Hay House, 2007)

Loving What Is, by Byron Katie with Stephen Mitchell (Three Rivers Press, 2003)

Mind to Matter: The Astonishing Science of How your Brain Creates Material Reality, by Dawson Church (Hay House, 2018)

Restful Sleep: The Complete Mind/Body Program for Overcoming Insomnia, by Deepak Chopra (Three Rivers House, 1994)

Super Brain: Unleashing the Explosive Power of Your Mind to Maximize Health, Happiness, and Spiritual Well-Being, by Deepak Chopra and Rudolph. E. Tanzi (Three Rivers Press, 2012)

The Attractor Factor: Five Easy Ways of Creating Wealth (or Anything Else) from the Inside Out, by Joe Vitale (Hypnotic Marketing Inc., 2009)

The EFT Manual, by Gary Craig (Energy Psychology Press, 2014)

The Genie in your Genes: Epigenetic Medicine and the New Biology of Intention, by Dawson Church (Hay House, 2015)

The Healing Self: A Revolutionary New Plan to Supercharge Your Immunity and Stay Well for Life, by Deepak Chopra and Rudolph. E. Tanzi (Harmony Books, 2018)

The Joy Diet: Ten Daily Practices for a Happier Life, by Martha Beck (Crown, 2003)

The Law and the Promise, by Neville Goddard

The Power Is Within You, by Louise L. Hay (Hay House Inc., 1991)

The Power of Now: A Guide to Spiritual Enlightenment, by Eckhart Tolle (New World Library, 2004)

The Power of Your Subconscious Mind, by Joseph Murphy

The Secret, by Rhonda Byrne (Atria Books/ Beyond Words, 2006)

The Self-Esteem Workbook, by Glenn R. Schiraldi (New Harbinger Publications, 2006)

The Tapping Solution: A Revolutionary System for Stress-Free Living, by Nick Ortner (Hay House, 2013)

The Tapping Solution for Manifesting Your Greatest Self, by Nick Ortner (Hay House, 2017)

The Tapping Solution for Parents, Children, and Teenagers, by Nick Ortner (Hay House, 2018)

AUDIO BOOKS

"NeuroWisdom: The New Brain Science of Money, Happiness, and Success," by Chris Manning and Mark Robert Waldman (Blackstone Audio, Inc., 2007)

"The Self- Esteem Workbook," by Glenn R. Schiraldi (New Harbinger Publications, 2006)

"The Ultimate Happiness Prescription: Seven Keys to Joy and Enlightenment," by Deepak Chopra (Random House Audio, 2009)

"You Can Heal your Life," by Louise L. Hay (Hay House, 1988)

WEBSITES

Dawson Church: EFT expert on Self-Love EFT Manual 3: 2018
https://www.youtube.com/watch?v=-UyiRgIxjVw

"Guided Meditations," by Deepak Chopra
https://chopra.com/articles/guided-meditations

"Guided Meditation to Manage Stress," by Deepak Chopra
https://www.youtube.com/watch?v=Eed-40vnCpo

"Harmonic Living" with EFT Practitioner Judy Lynne
Mindset Development & Law of Attraction Coach
CEO Harmonic Living Now
https://harmoniclivingnow.com

"How to Tap for Beginners," with Nick Ortner
https://www.youtube.com/watch?v=XRfLTQjJhp0

"Law of Attraction," by Abraham-Hicks Publications
https://www.abraham-hicks.com

"Love Yourself Unconditionally–First Chakra"/ Insight Timer
https://insighttimer.com/suzannelie/guided-meditations/love-yourself-unconditionally~first-chakra

"Master of Living Meditation Programs" with Jessi Rita Hoffman
(one-on-one instruction via phone or Skype)
www.MasterOfLivingMeditations.com

"Neurogym," by John Assaraf, CEO of Neurogym
https://www.youtube.com/channel/UCIomhMJjpMOTRepsEP_X
qlA

The Option Method (for choosing happiness)
http://www.choosehappiness.net

The Tapping Place by Dawson Church
(a list of EFT Universe certified practitioners available 24/7)
https://www.eftuniverse.com/landing/the-tapping-place

"Unsinkable Bounce-Back System," by Sonia Ricotti
https://soniaricotti.com/

TED TALKS

"Become Who You Really Are," by Andrea Pennington/ TEDxIUM
https://www.youtube.com/watch?v=5pW2b1vwwf4

"Designing For Generosity" by Nipun Mehta / TEDxBerkeley
https://www.youtube.com/watch?v=kpyc84kamhw

"Inspired Action," by Abraham/ Esther Hicks
https://ed.ted.com/on/fgmh3ly4

"Knowing Your Worth," by Fardousa Jama/ TEDx Gustavus Adolphus College
https://youtu.be/F5yvoSu2OV0

"Meet Yourself: A User's Guide to Building Self-Esteem," by Niko Everett/ TEDxYouth@ Bommer Canyon
https://www.youtube.com/watch?list=PLIarbzft73-NavAxoM6_uVknzjsNSbbLz&v=uOrzmFUJtrs

"Removing Negative Self-Talk," by Abria Joseph/ TEDx Youth@NIST
https://www.youtube.com/watch?v=teVE3VGrBhM

"Stop Sabotaging Yourself," by Debi Silber/ TEDx Fulton Street
https://www.youtube.com/watch?v=XX30i6nC7ro

"The Art of Being Yourself," by Caroline McHugh/ TEDx Milton Keynes Women
https://www.youtube.com/watch?v=veEQQ-N9xWU

FOUNDATIONS

Art of Living Foundation
A nonprofit international, humanitarian, and educational organization in over a hundred and fifty cities. It teaches meditation and breathing techniques (Sudarshan Kriya) to calm the mind and body.
www.artofliving.com

Dove Self-Esteem Project
This foundation educates parents, teachers, youth leaders, and mentors in how to foster self-esteem in youth.
https://www.dove.com/us/en/dove-self-esteem-project.html

Emotional Freedom Technique (EFT)
Gary Craig, the founder of EFT, offers this free, downloadable manual that explains the technique of tapping.
https://www.emofree.com/

Landmark Worldwide Foundation
A forum aimed at bringing about self-confidence in one's personal and professional life.
http://www.landmarkworldwide.com/

National Association for Self-Esteem (NASE)
NASE's goal is to integrate self-esteem into American society so that no matter what their age or background, every individual can experience personal worth and happiness.
http://healthyselfesteem.org

Sathya Sai International Organization
A non-denominational, voluntary organization. Its members come from all faiths. It promotes personal responsibility for ethical transformation through selfless love and service.
http://www.sathyasai.org

Service Space
Service Space is an organization run by volunteers that leverages technology to encourage everyday people around the world to do small acts of service. It's aim is to ignite the fundamental generosity in people, creating both inner and outer transformation.
https://www.servicespace.org

The Canfield Training Group
Guides you through a ten-day program in "The Success Principle," aimed at raising self-esteem and helping you to achieve whatever you want to do or to be.
www.jackcanfield.com

RETREATS

https://www.bookyogaretreats.com/
Well-rated yoga retreats from two days to more than two weeks found all over the world. Various kinds of yoga: Sweat and Flow, Mindfulness Meditation, Remove and Revitalize, and Fitness and Strength offered at different skill levels (beginner, intermediate, or advanced)

https://www.prajnayoga.net
Tias and Surya Little offer yoga retreats in New Mexico and many other places. They also offer an online course: "Elevate your Chakras" on www.YogaGlow.com

APPS FOR MEDITATION

Calm
Offers a selection of three- to twenty-five-minute calming sessions (the playing of soothing sounds) and a ten-minute mindfulness program to start or end the day. Also offers breathing exercises, and soothing sounds to improve your sleep.
https://www.calm.com/meditate

Headspace
A mindfulness meditation app that is ideal for beginners. Its free trial of ten exercises helps you learn how to do mindfulness meditation and apply it to your life.
https://www.headspace.com

Insight Timer
This is my favorite app as there is such a variety of guided meditations—over four thousand from numerous meditation practitioners. Different guided meditations target different things, such as better sleep, chakra clearing, or relaxation. To listen offline, you can purchase a monthly subscription. Here is a guided meditation for loving yourself:
https://insighttimer.com/suzannelie/guided-meditations/love-yourself-unconditionally~first-chakra
https://insighttimer.com

Stop, Breathe, and Think
This app offers a great feature where it asks you in a short survey how you feel emotionally, mentally, and physically, then offers customized guided meditations according to your answers. Various guided meditations help you with various things, such as breathing mindfully, sleeping better, tracking your mood and progress, or staying motivated. Useful for beginners all the way to advanced meditators.
https://itunes.apple.com/us/app/stop-breathe-think/id778848692?mt=8

APP FOR TAPPING

The Tapping Solution App
Over one hundred "tapping meditations" to get relief from stress-related challenges. Daily inspirational, motivational and insightful quotes. Visual tapping-point graphics to keep you on track during each tapping meditation.
www.thetappingsolution.com/blog/tapping-solution-app

BELL APPS

Buddhists have a practice of ringing a bell at intervals to remind them to gather their mind from straying thoughts. In the same way, a bell app may be used to ground and center yourself and refocus your energy. This mindfulness app helps bring your mind back to your body to be aware of being in the now. Breathe three times, relax, and observe mindfully; when the bell goes off again, resume what you were doing. This habit helps train you to be aware of what your state of mind is.

Bell of Mindfulness
Platform: Chrome browser
You can set a mindfulness bell timer to ring at intervals of five minutes to an hour.
Chrome: https://bit.ly/2sN0luW

Insight Timer
Listed in the Apps for Meditation section, this app also has the ability to play a variety of bell sounds.
https://insighttimer.com

Mind Bell
You have the option of setting a mindfulness bell reminder as often you want, or you can set the phone to vibrate instead of playing the bell sound. The notification feature is helpful.
https://www.dknapps.de/mindbell/index.html

Mindful Mynah
You can set the time interval you prefer and choose from a range of sounds. The "fuzzy reminders" feature helps you set any number of random bells which you would like to have ring within the hour.
https://42burnside.com/mindful-mynah/

Praise

"Geetanjali gracefully shares of her own experience, small personal practices that can help us go deeper into ourselves, uncovering vitality and a natural gratefulness and desire to give to others. While our "recipes" will artfully vary, You Are the Cake reminds us to walk towards the doorsteps of deep equanimity, so love can arise effortlessly within our consciousness."

Nipun Mehta & Christopher Johnnidis
Founder Service Space, Dalai Lama's Unsung Hero of Compassion
(& C Johnnidis - Service Space)

"This book offers smart pathways towards understanding self-love, acceptance, forgiveness and being worthy of yourself."

Sarah M. McKay DPhil (Oxon)
Neuroscientist, Founder of Neuroscience Academy,
Author of 'The Women's Brain Book - the neuroscience of health, hormones and happiness' (Hachette)
www.yourbrainhealth.com.au ~ www.theneuroacademy.com
Vice President of Australasian Medical Writers Association (AMWA)

"An excellent reading of hope, love and positive energy for all of us and especially for all that have difficult and challenging health and life issues. Your words taught me how to slow down and breath and be patient with mind and body. Thank you for giving us this magnificent piece of art, heart and soul to enlighten our own lives while sharing your own."

Linda Tannenbaum
Founder and CEO/President
Open Medicine Foundation® (OMF)
www.omf.ngo
650-242-8669 office; 818-231-6994 mobile
Leading research. Delivering hope.

"This book leads the reader into a deep understanding of the truth of who they are in totality through evidence-based research and real-life stories. Geetanjali gives powerful examples of how our beliefs, thoughts and emotions can either devastate or empower us. She humbly shares the years of pain she endured and the awakening, techniques and processes she used to heal her own life and create a life of peace, love and true happiness. If you are tired of just existing, feeling stuck, unworthy or unhappy and you're ready to fall in love with yourself and with life, then you're in good hands with Geetanjali's 'YOU ARE THE CAKE'!"

Judy Lynne
Mindset Development & Law of Attraction Coach,
CEO Harmonic Living Now

154

Acknowledgements

Writing this book has been a great journey for me, and I am grateful to the Divine for giving me guidance, wisdom, and encouragement to impart the message of self-love to all.

Deep thanks for all things electronic go out to Arun, my husband, who I fondly call my tech-guru, and to my children, Amit Arunkumar and Priyanka Arunkumar, who have always been at my side with unwavering faith. Thanks to Sofie Singer, my daughter-in-law, for her continued enthusiasm, and to Jason Avery for his encouragement. This book could not have the spirit it has without the invaluable support of my affectionate father, Fatu Thadani; my brother Vijay Thadani, who placed confidence in me; and caring Bina Thadani. A big hug to my furry friend and soul supporter Einstein, who sat by me patiently. Thanks to my darling mother, Jamuna Thadani, who smiles from above and has been the guiding light in my life. I am grateful to each one of you. You brighten up my days.

To my friends, who make up the fabric of my life, thank you for your endless support and faith in me through this literary journey. In no particular order: Vidya Belkhale, Shashi Patel, Laurie Shimizu, Rita Ramakabir, Vandi Thirumale, Asha Vis, Jayashree Rajendran, Ragini Srinivasan, Milan Bikhchandani, Mukta Mukhija, Meena Oza, Asha Bijj, Sandya Iyer, Shilpa Padwekar, Sujatha Narayan, Neelu Acharya, Sunita Ferreira, Jayshree Sundar, Ranjana Sivaram, Olivia D'Costa, Sujata Desai, Neeti Bopparai, Linda Tannenbaum, Keeirthi Lunawat,

Shweta Thakur, R. Sundar, and so many more, including my extended family, merigang.

My sincere gratitude to Raka Gupta, my supporter, friend, and Photoshop wizard, for cheering me on. I am indebted to my marketing team, friends, my book club, Anuj Changvi, and Leila Chaudhry, for their support.

I am grateful to Demi Bernice Eslit, for the wonderful cover design.

To all the amazing teachers and experts whose wisdom is captured in this book, my sincere thanks. I keep growing and learning from your work. Gratitude to John Assaraf, Mark Robert Waldman, Sarah McKay, Sonia Ricotti, Dawson Church, Gary Craig, and Nick Ortner.

To all my readers, may I express my gratitude for the gift of your time and interest in reading this book. May you continue to grow and blossom and revel in your sweetness.

About the Author

Geetanjali Arunkumar is passionate about inspiring people to love themselves, which she believes is core to building one's self-esteem and living happily.

She holds a degree in psychology from the University of Mumbai. Geetanjali enjoys contributing articles and editorials to magazines and for research funding.

She is a certified yoga teacher and a professional artist who has displayed her work at numerous shows.

Geetanjali Arunkumar is the mother of two wonderful children that she raised in spite of life's challenges. She was diagnosed with a chronic debilitating illness at a young age, which she learned to overcome by applying the techniques she shares in this book. Much of her writing comes from her own experiences and from counseling others who have reached out to her.

Visit her website at
www.urthecake.com or www.geetanjaliarunkumar.com

Join her on Facebook at www.facebook.com/gaauthor
Find her on Instagram at www.instagram.com/urthecake
Follow her on Twitter at www.twitter.com/urthecake

She would appreciate it if you could please take a moment and leave a balanced review on your platform of choice.

Made in the USA
San Bernardino, CA
03 November 2019